When Your Child is Hurting

Glynnis Whitwer

HARVEST HOUSE PUBLISHERS

EUGENE, OREGON

Unless otherwise indicated, all Scripture quotations are taken from the HOLY BIBLE, NEW INTER-NATIONAL VERSION®. NIV®. Copyright © 1973, 1978, 1984 by the International Bible Society. Used by permission of Zondervan. All rights reserved.

Verses marked NLT are taken from the *Holy Bible,* New Living Translation, copyright © 1996, 2004. Used by permission of Tyndale House Publishers, Inc., Wheaton, IL 60189 USA. All rights reserved.

Verses marked NASB are taken from the New American Standard Bible®, © 1960, 1962, 1963, 1968, 1971, 1972, 1973, 1975, 1977, 1995 by The Lockman Foundation. Used by permission. (www.Lockman.org)

Verses marked RSV are taken from the Revised Standard Version of the Bible, copyright © 1946, 1952, 1971 by the Division of Christian Education of the National Council of the Churches of Christ in the U.S.A. Used by permission. All rights reserved.

Verses marked NKJV are taken from the New King James Version. Copyright © 1982 by Thomas Nelson, Inc. Used by permission. All rights reserved.

Verses marked NCV are taken from *The Holy Bible, New Century Version,* Copyright © 1987, 1988, 1991 by Word Publishing, Nashville, TN 37214. Used by permission.

Cover by Left Coast Design, Portland, Oregon

Cover photo © Image Source / Getty Images

WHEN YOUR CHILD IS HURTING
Copyright © 2009 by Glynnis Whitwer
Published by Harvest House Publishers
Eugene, Oregon 97402
www.harvesthousepublishers.com

Library of Congress Cataloging-in-Publication Data
Whitwer, Glynnis, 1961-
When your child is hurting / Glynnis Whitwer.
   p. cm.
ISBN 978-0-7369-2463-4 (pbk.)
1. Child rearing—Religious aspects—Christianity. 2. Suffering in children. I. Title.
BV4529.W553 2009
248.8'45—dc22

2008049430

Printed in the United States of America

09 10 11 12 13 14 15 16 17 / DP-SK / 10 9 8 7 6 5 4 3 2 1

This book is lovingly dedicated
to my firstborn, Joshua O. Whitwer.
Though you have faced many hurts in your life,
your joyful outlook on life is a testimony
to God's loving protection over your heart.
Thank you for letting me tell your stories in this book
and for being the first "testing ground,"
as your dad and I try to figure out this thing called parenthood.
May you continue to follow hard after Jesus.
I love you.
Mom

Acknowledgments

Writing this book has been a difficult experience. I have relived much of my own childhood sadnesses and cried new tears for those my children experienced. Yet, there has been joy in the writing. God reminds me constantly of His compassion, help, and hope. He sees every hurt, and He saves every tear. We follow a God who cares intimately for the pain we experience, and in His perfect plan, He has an answer and a healing for every hurt. For that I am forever grateful.

I am very thankful to the parents and children who have allowed me to share their stories in this book. Every story has been approved by the child (who may now be an adult), and I have been impressed by their willingness to help others through their own experiences. You are each shining examples of God's love in action. My thanks to the following friends: Amy and Jason Beck, Gavin and Ronin Beck, Sue and Larry Eickman, Jordan Eickman, Sean Flanigan, Ann Guthery, Marlo Francis, Ben Francis, Barb and Tim Frey, Hannah Frey, Paula and David Gray, Jody and Bud Kingston, Jennifer Kingston, Cheri Nace, and Sarah Peppel.

My deepest thanks to my husband, Tod, who never once wavered in his support and love for me, and our five blessings: Joshua, Dylan, Robbie, Cathrine, and Ruth. Thank you for allowing me to share in your life and to share your stories with others.

Thank you to the friends who helped proofread my manuscript: My first friend ever—my mother—Kathryn Owens, Paula Gray, Beth Blake, and Ana Stine.

To my dear friends at Proverbs 31 Ministries—Jesus sent His disciples out in twos for a reason. God surely intended life and ministry to be done together. I love you all and thank you for your ongoing love and support.

To the staff at Harvest House—what I have observed for years from the outside has been confirmed from the inside. Your passion for producing God-honoring books and advancing the kingdom of God is reaping a harvest of changed lives. Thank you for allowing me the privilege of linking arms in ministry with you. A special thank you to Terry Glaspey for challenging me to press on and make this book better and for your compassion for children who are hurt. God surely hand-picked Peggy Wright as my editor—thank you!

To Jesus, who makes life worth living and offers a hope beyond what we see—I love You.

Contents

Introduction

It was a busy Saturday afternoon, and our family was running errands in the car. From the passenger seat, I turned to chat with the kids and noticed my middle son, Dylan, wearing a baseball cap his younger brother, Robbie, had purchased earlier in the week. When I asked about the switch in ownership, Dylan said Robbie gave him the hat. Curious to know the reason, I nonchalantly asked Robbie why he had done that. No response came from the back seat.

This wasn't just any hat. Robbie purchased it at a very special outing earlier in the week, when he and his big brother Josh attended a Christian concert as part of a church outing. A white mesh trucker hat of sorts, I wouldn't have picked it, but it was cool at that moment to my fifth-grade son. Proud as could be, Robbie wore this white mesh cap to school the next day. Now Dylan owned the hat.

I repeated the question, thinking Robbie hadn't heard me. When I still didn't get a response, I turned in my seat to see Robbie with his head down, face contorted, tears running down his cheeks and valiantly trying to suppress sobs. It was just a simple question about a hat...at least that's what I initially thought.

It took Robbie a few moments to compose himself. When he did, he stammered, "Someone said I looked stupid in my hat."

When we heard Robbie's tearful response, two things immediately and simultaneously happened. His two older brothers chimed in to tell him how cool he looked in the hat and to ignore those types of comments. At the same time, I was plotting how to hunt down this rude child who spoke thoughtless and unkind words to my baby boy. Thankfully my children chose the higher moral path, and Robbie resumed ownership of the hat.

Reflecting on that incident, I realize how often my pain interferes with the help I might give my children as they struggle to overcome the everyday offenses of life. My gut level response is often to wrap my arms around my child to protect him or her from further hurt. Quite honestly I often simmer with resentment and anger over the cause of their pain. Neither one of those responses prepare my children for dealing with the inevitable hurt they'll experience on life's journey.

Inside every child is a tender heart that suffers bumps and bruises from the hurts of life. Ask any adult what hurt her as a child, and waves of stories flow. We remember the harsh response of a coach, the reprimand of a teacher, and a critical observation from a family member. We remember standing on the sidelines, being teased about our weight, or being left out of a birthday party. When faced with our child's pain, those memories can return to the surface, clouding our judgment and limiting our effectiveness to help.

Obviously you are a parent who cares deeply about your child. I commend you for investing in your parenting skills, your family, and your child by reading this book. As you begin, I want to share a few things that might help you understand my approach in writing this book. My goals for this book are twofold:

- To equip parents with practical and biblical ways to help their children overcome the everyday hurts of life.

- Through helping parents, I pray children will be equipped to be confident and obedient followers of God throughout their lives.

As the mother of five children, I have lived out many of these hurts with my children, and you'll read about them throughout the book. As a sort of an introduction, you might like to know that God chose to grow our family through the birth of three sons, Joshua, Dylan, and

Robbie, and later through the adoption of two daughters, Cathrine and Ruth. My husband and I believe each child was hand-picked by God to be ours—in His perfect timing and manner. In some of the stories, you'll read about the three boys alone, but that's just because our daughters weren't part of our family at that specific time. Please know that every story has their full approval. What they didn't approve, you'll never read.

I also am writing from the experience of being a past senior high youth leader, camp counselor, children's ministry director and volunteer, and teacher and leader in parenting ministry. I have served children and their parents in the church for over half my life.

What you didn't notice in that list of experiences was any medical or psychological practice. Hence, this book is not written from that perspective, nor is it meant to address the more serious issues children face. You will find professionals quoted, but the heart of this book is practical experience from one mom to another. I believe parents know their children better than anyone else does. Trust your judgment and intuition and don't let anyone undermine your confidence.

However, if you find yourself dealing with an issue that feels above your ability, it probably is. I would encourage you to seek counsel from Christian professionals, who should be able to help from a biblical perspective. The reader should not use this book to answer concerns regarding serious medical or psychological issues.

There is one more point I should make. I have discovered two critically important components of parenting: prayer and knowing God's Word. Prayer and Scripture orient me to God's wisdom and truth when circumstances threaten to overwhelm me. I could have included these two items in every chapter, they are that important. However, you probably would have wondered why you didn't just buy a book on prayer and Bible study. Hence, I haven't explored them in detail. Please know those two practices are the heartbeat of successful parenting.

With that I invite you to read this book in its entirety or read a chapter based on your child's current need. Each chapter includes stories of how other parents dealt with similar issues and offers specific biblically-based encouragement and practical advice. The chapters also include Scripture memory verses for children and parents, inspirational quotes, and a Bible study that you can complete in a group, with an older child, or as a personal devotion. Many of the questions will delve into your heart because as parents we can't take our children any further than we have gone ourselves.

May God bless you richly for taking this step to help your children. May His Spirit speak truth into your hearts, encourage you when you feel weak, and inspire you to press on in your parenting. And may you fall even deeper in love with Jesus and your children.

In His Love,

Glynnis

Chapter One

The Difference a Parent Makes

*I wish I may, I wish I might, have
the wish I wish tonight.*

Joshua Owen Whitwer joined our family as a healthy nine-pound, two-ounce baby boy. Being first-time parents, we navigated the new world of parenting like two lost explorers reading an upside-down map. Between naïveté and sleep exhaustion, we stumbled and bumbled our way through those first few weeks. The emotional highs and lows were startling. One moment my heart overflowed with joy and amazement at the miracle of our child. The next, panic and fear threatened my peace.

The reality that we were responsible for the life of a helpless child weighed heavy on our minds. *Is the crib safe enough? Should Joshua lie on his back or his side? Is he too hot or too cold? Is he getting enough to eat? Or too much?* My sweet baby seemed so vulnerable and helpless. The insecurities of being a mother plagued me daily.

A Mama Bear Emerges

I'll never forget one of our first days at home when those worries turned into a commitment. I rested in a recliner with Joshua in my arms and looked around my house. It surprised me that even with all of our pre-baby preparations, many things looked potentially danger-ous from this new perspective. I particularly worried about our two dogs. Although gentle and loving, their large sizes seemed overpow-ering. The fear started as a cold rock in the pit of my stomach and radiated throughout my body. Panic overwhelmed me, and sobs tore from my chest. I clutched Joshua tighter and vowed to protect him with my life. I already loved him beyond measure, but at that moment, I became his defender of all threats—seen and unseen.

Looking back now, I realize my meltdown had two sides. In part, God gave me a healthy and loving maternal instinct. Joshua did need parents to defend and protect him. I did need to ensure a safe environment for my son. But the unhealthy part, motivated by irrational fear, did not come from God. This fear of the unknown alternately paralyzed me and then turned me into a primeval, protective mama bear. I quickly assumed a no-one's-gonna-mess-with-my-child attitude and quietly upped my cautious and protective approach to motherhood.

Joshua was a very happy baby who loved and accepted everyone. Taking him to church or other outings brought a myriad of comments about his sweet smile. Joshua's gentle personality made him an easygoing baby. My husband, Tod, and I enjoyed each step in his development and thanked God daily for this gift. Being a big baby, Joshua progressed slightly ahead of each developmental milestone with one exception—his vision. At six months old, we noticed Joshua didn't seem to focus on things well, and one eye turned slightly in. A trip to the doctor's office set our minds at ease when the pediatrician told us most babies' eyes turn in slightly. Unfortunately the doctor was wrong. Joshua's vision didn't correct itself, and at 11 months, we found ourselves sitting in a pediatric ophthalmologist's office, receiving a prescription for glasses and being warned of the probability of surgery.

I held it together in the doctor's office but fell apart on the way home. How could my precious baby wear glasses before he could walk? What would surgery mean? Would he lose his vision? Could he die on the operating table? Fear enveloped me like an icy cold fog. The future was uncertain as far as my child's vision, but my commitment to protect Joshua was ragingly certain. I had already decided to become a protector of my child's physical well-being, now I envisioned myself as his emotional protector—able to fend off the inevitable taunts from children who would make fun of him for his thick-lensed glasses.

At 18 months of age, Joshua did need strabismus surgery to help correct his vision. That helped some, but powerful glasses and daily patching of his strong eye for many years completed the program. Even with those efforts, Joshua's corrected vision today is only 20/25.

On the outside I looked like a normal mother. On the inside I felt like a hypervigilant mess. Constantly on the alert for any potential harm to Joshua, even a curious look from a stranger raised my protective antenna. A comment from another child about Joshua's glasses or patch elicited my swoop-and-grab escape plan. I grew weary caring for all my child's needs and protecting him from any hurt, both real and imagined. But it was worth it to me.

Our New Reality

I successfully protected Joshua to the best of my ability for years. I controlled his whereabouts, his companions, and what he saw. Life was good. Two other beautiful babies joined our family, and Joshua loved his little brothers. In turn they loved him back. In fact they adored him for his kindness and loving nature. None of the threats I had envisioned entered our world. My confidence as a mother had increased, and although having three little boys challenged me in many ways, I felt good about my role as protector. However, this idyllic life changed in a day. Although most people would not define what happened as a true catastrophe, it shocked us out of the sheltered life I created for my children. In a word it was "school."

The day Joshua entered kindergarten, I came to an abrupt realization of our new reality: Joshua had moved beyond my ability to protect him. I couldn't protect him physically. And I couldn't protect him emotionally. For five hours a day, other children surrounded Joshua, and they didn't love him like his little brothers and I did. A teacher oversaw his daily activities, as she also cared for 20 other children. He was on a playground without me watching. Even though it was a Christian school, Joshua spent his day with children whose parents raised them with different guidelines than we had at home.

As the truth of this new reality seeped into my life and smeared my makeup with many salty tears, I realized I had to find another way to help Joshua. I really wanted to hide my little boy under my wings so no one would ever touch him, but I knew that wasn't an option. As I wrestled with this desire to protect at all costs, God started speaking gently to me about two very specific issues. The first was trust. God asked me a question He continues to ask me today: *Do you just say you trust Me, or do you really trust Me?*

Do You Really Trust Me?

God asked me a defining question for my life; one that I had to settle in my heart. Do I trust Him with the life of my children, or do I just say I do. I love my children so much—it's hard to imagine anyone loving them more. God was reminding me that not only does He love them more than I, but He also has the ability to protect them when I can't. Entrusting my children to God took me to an entirely new level of faith. For me it was where the rubber met the proverbial road. It wasn't enough to talk about trusting God, I actually had to do it.

So every day when I lovingly combed Joshua's hair, dressed him in his little shorts and T-shirt, and drove him to school, I prayed. Actually it was more like a desperate begging plea: *God, please protect my Joshua.* Every time fear rose up in my heart, I had to (and still do today) repeat this prayer: *I choose to trust You, God. I don't want to just say I trust You—I actually want to trust You.*

Through this question, God revealed that my self-sufficiency was in fact pride. I assumed a role God never meant for me, and through that role, I took God's place in the life of my child. The truth is I am a woefully imperfect and inadequate substitute for such a holy, perfect, and powerful Savior. When I assumed responsibility for my child's complete protection, I was in fact training my son to look to me for answers and not God.

My overprotective approach to parenting not only hindered my own faith in God, it was potentially influencing the faith of my child. God showed me I had to deal with the issue of faith before I would ever be free of the fear that had shadowed me for years. Even more importantly, my children need to learn to turn to God when they have a problem. The second issue God dealt with me about was preparing my child to effectively deal with life and all its inevitable problems.

Prepare and Protect

One of my mother's best gifts to me was teaching me to be a problem solver. It's because she was and is one of the best problem solvers I know. If I had a school project to tackle, she taught me how to break down the components and address them one by one. She equipped me with tools and techniques that still benefit me today.

I realized I had to teach my own children to be problem solvers. By trying to protect them from any problems, I was in fact thwarting their ability to become independent. Instead God showed me I needed to prepare my kids to deal with problems because trouble will arrive on their doorsteps throughout their entire lives.

My pastor has a saying: You are either just getting out of trouble, you are currently in trouble, or you are just about to get into trouble. Trouble in life is inevitable. I did my children a disservice by trying to protect them from trouble because I could only do so for a short time. I learned, during those early parenting years, that teaching children to effectively deal with trouble and hurt, instead of how to avoid it, was actually beneficial. Dealing with pain correctly is spring training for adulthood.

Why Allow Some Pain?

Because of his academic success in elementary school, our son Dylan qualified to test for the international baccalaureate program at his high school. In one of the parent information meetings, the advisor for the program confessed that it is a difficult program. Not every student fits in the program, and she wanted us to know that right up front. However, she advised, the challenge can be good for a disciplined and hard-working high school student.

With college-aged students of her own, she knows the shock many college freshmen get when they leave the protective oversight of their parents' care and enter the stark independence of college life. Many young adults face a brick wall for the first time in their lives and do so alone. The counselor invited us to consider this program as an opportunity for a young adult to face that brick wall while still having his or her parent's full support.

In other words, by knowingly allowing our son to face some difficult challenges now, we could strategically position ourselves to help him deal with them. This high school program could be an opportunity for more than a better education. If approached with the right attitude, it could prepare Dylan to face challenges in the future.

As I reflected on the words of the guidance counselor, I realized God had been teaching me and weaving this philosophy through my parenting for years. Dr. James Dobson puts it this way, "I would remind you that the human personality grows through mild adversity, provided it is not crushed in the process. Contrary to what you might believe, the ideal environment for your child is not one devoid of problems and trials."[1]

Allowing some pain to enter our children's lives also teaches them to turn to God. If a child's life is free from all pain, she can easily miss her need for God. Although this seems paradoxical, I have experienced this in my own life. It is in times of deep pain and suffering that I seek God's peace, and God responds by settling in close. God teaches me things about Himself that I would never learn in the easy time.

The times when things are going smoothly are the times I deceptively think I have life under control. At those times I neglect to seek God's help and miss tremendous blessings. While I never seek out pain to grow closer to God, I'm thankful He can use pain to reveal Himself to me.

The Transfer of Responsibility

This idea of preparing a child for inevitable hurts involves a partnership between child and parent. This partnership starts with holding hands and facing a problem together and gently progresses to full independent problem solving. As God models standing by us at all times, we should be our children's teacher in the transfer of responsibility. I saw this lesson in action one day on my front porch.

I opened the front door one spring afternoon to discover an adorable blond-haired preschooler standing by a woman who looked like her mother. The little girl's right hand hung at her side, clutching a few flowers that looked suspiciously like those from our front yard.

"Hi," the woman nervously said. "My daughter has something she needs to say to you."

The little girl hung her head and spoke no words. It only took me a few seconds to assess the situation and step out onto the porch. The silence lengthened. I glanced compassionately at the mother, whose eyes were pooling with tears. I knew she wanted to intervene but wisely held back.

I dropped to one knee in front of the child and held her flower-filled hand in mine. "Did you pick those flowers from my garden?" I asked. With her head still down, she nodded. "Did you pick them for your mommy?" I continued.

Her head lifted. She nodded and whispered, "I'm sorry."

Tears now streamed down the mother's face as she obviously felt every ounce of her child's fear and discomfort. This was harder on the mother than the child, but the little girl did what she needed to do. I profusely thanked that dear child for her apology and commended her on her love for her mother. The two of them left my door hand-in-hand, and God rewarded me with a beautiful picture of a parent helping to prepare a child for the reality of life.

As we help our children deal with hurt and pain in their lives, sometimes we hold their hands as they walk through it. Our physical and emotional presence is healthy and right, especially for young children. Whether it's facing a challenging assignment at school, a difficult friend, or the loss of a pet, sometimes we need to be standing right next to our child, an arm draped around his shoulder. At other times, as our child matures in both age and experience, we can slowly transition the responsibility for facing challenges. Instead of standing right next to him, we might be just outside the door.

Then the day will come when our son or daughter deals with the problem independently. If we are still holding our teenager's hand when she auditions for a part in a play, we've missed some opportunities for training along the way. If we do our jobs right as parents, we will transition from hand holder to coach to counselor. Then our children will consult us as needed.

Making an Eternal Difference

On my worst days as a parent, I feel like a referee without a whistle. I'm exhausted by the number of sibling conflicts to judge, frustrated by calling foul on someone who should have known better, and ready to sit *myself* on the bench to rest! Those are the days when success as a parent means no injuries.

On my best days as a parent, my heart overflows with gratitude that God entrusted me with raising five of His children. Instead of being discouraged, God grants me a peek at His plans for my kids and the importance of my role. When I see my son playing guitar in the worship band or when my daughter prays for me, that glimpse of the future sustains me through the dark times. On those days, I grasp the value and worth of parenting and the positive influence my husband and I can be.

It's also on those days when I'm encouraged to pursue one of my top goals as a Christian parent, which is to raise children who will love and follow hard after Jesus on their own. Amazingly it is in the difficult, challenging, and painful times that God gives us opportunities to direct our children to Him. He is ready and willing to reveal Himself personally to them. It is in the midst of the pain our children learn that God is more than a character in a storybook. He is a God who desires a personal relationship with them.

You see I have not learned to trust God in the good times. Oh, I love Him easily in the good times. I'm thankful in the good times. But I have learned to *trust* God in the bad times. It's in the hard times, when I cry out for help, that I experience His miraculous intervention. It's in the lonely times, when I cry in despair, that I am comforted by

His presence. It's in the fearful times, when I pray for peace, that I am overwhelmed with His protective presence.

I haven't learned to trust God from reading a great book. I haven't learned to trust God by listening to an amazing sermon. I haven't learned to trust God by hearing how my friend trusts God. No. I have learned to trust God by experiencing something difficult, by stepping out in faith and obedience, and finding out for myself that He is trustworthy.

We can give this same "gift" to our children. We can actually help them experience the reality of God in their own lives by how we coach them through hurt and trouble. I believe we serve a God who longs to intervene in our lives when given the invitation. What better time to experience the power and majesty of God than when a child is young.

The Reality and Hope of Life

While I still wish I could protect my children from all harm, I know that's not possible. Job 5:7 says, "Yet man is born to trouble as surely as sparks fly upward." Even the Son of God experienced hurt and pain while on this earth. Avoiding hurt isn't an option. However, teaching children to deal effectively and independently with pain is possible.

Allowing children to develop independent thoughts and actions is a natural part of growing up—as painful as it is at times. With four teenagers in the house right now, I sometimes long for simpler days when I made all the decisions. But that's not the reality of growing up. Kids need to make their own decisions to develop confidence and maturity. When faced with a dilemma of any kind, children need to learn how to process the situation, consider options, make a decision, and then learn from the consequences. This is how we become wise and confident adults.

Throughout the rest of this book, it is my hope that as we discover how to help our children deal with the everyday hurts of life, we will be raising them to be children who turn to God as the ultimate source of wisdom and strength. With this foundation, it is my prayer that they will become adults who do the same. The truth is there is no other answer to the problems in this world besides God, and the most important decision our children ever have to make is what to do with Jesus.

Instead of looking at problems as something to avoid, may those problems be opportunities for our children to understand their need for a Savior and for God to prove His faithfulness. We have a promise from the mouth of Jesus Himself regarding this: "In this world you will have trouble. But take heart! I have overcome the world" (John 16:33). Praise God there is hope!

Memory Verses

Therefore put on the full armor of God, so that when the day of evil comes, you may be able to stand your ground, and after you have done everything, to stand.

EPHESIANS 6:13

Fathers, do not provoke your children to anger by the way you treat them. Rather, bring them up with the discipline and instruction that comes from the Lord.

EPHESIANS 6:4 NLT

Children are a gift from the LORD; they are a reward from him.

PROVERBS 127:3 NLT

Jesus said, "Let the little children come to me, and do not hinder them, for the kingdom of heaven belongs to such as these."

MATTHEW 19:14

Whoever welcomes one of these little children in
my name welcomes me; and whoever welcomes me
does not welcome me but the one who sent me.

MARK 9:37

Encouraging Words

Making the decision to have a child is momentous.
It is to decide forever to have your heart go
walking around outside your body.

—ELIZABETH STONE

Before I got married I had six theories about bringing
up children; now I have six children, and no theories.

—JOHN WILMOT

To bring up a child in the way he should go,
travel that way yourself once in a while.

—JOSH BILLINGS

Don't worry that children never listen to you;
worry that they are always watching you.

—ROBERT FULGHUM

Likely as not, the child you can do the least
with will do the most to make you proud.

—MIGNON MCLAUGHLIN

Discussion or Journal Questions

1. What is the greatest parenting challenge you are personally facing right now?

2. Where do you turn for support or encouragement to face parenting challenges? Is it meeting your needs?

3. Proverbs 22:6 says, "Train a child in the way he should go, and when he is old he will not turn from it." In what ways are you training your child right now?

4. In your opinion what are the three most important character traits a parent needs to effectively raise children?

5. Describe why each of these traits is important.

6. Are there any character traits you believe you need to help parent your child? If so, write those down.

7. When someone hurts your child, what is normally your first reaction? How does that reaction help or hurt?

8. What are some of the biggest challenges facing children today?

9. What have you learned from your heavenly Father that has helped you be a better parent?

10. As you begin this book, what is one prayer you have for yourself? What is one prayer you have for your child? (If you have more than one child, identify a prayer for each.)

Chapter Two

Dealing with Disappointment

Rain, rain go away...

I waited anxiously on the sidewalk while my seventh-grade son walked to the band room. Josh tried to act nonchalant, but I could tell he was excited. A letter awaited him, informing us of his acceptance or rejection to the school's top jazz band. I held my breath as he returned, holding a sealed white envelope.

Josh had been preparing for weeks to audition for Jazz I. From the day he received the music, he rushed home from school to rehearse. Josh already had jazz band experience, as he'd been playing in Jazz II, the school's beginning jazz band, for two years. We were all excited about his potential to advance.

There was only one spot for his instrument, the bass guitar, and Josh knew he had competition from another strong bass player who'd already played in Jazz I for a year. At the audition on Friday, Josh was ready and played his best. It was an agonizing wait over the weekend, but Monday finally came and with it the announcement of who made the band.

We both grinned as Josh ripped into the envelope, anticipation making us silly. But Josh's face told it all as he opened the letter to discover he hadn't made the top band. Discouragement washed away the hopes and dreams of a moment earlier. He schooled his features quickly to reflect acceptance, but I saw the depth of his pain. As a consolation, the teacher said she would reserve his spot in the lower band if he was interested.

I forced a bright smile, told him I was proud of his effort, and hugged him goodbye. Josh turned and walked toward his classroom, with his shoulders hunched and a slow step. Feeling hot tears burn my eyes, I quickly turned to walk back home before Josh could see the emotion threatening to overflow. My heart ached because of his sadness; not only his, but mine too. I couldn't stop the tears as I remembered the sports teams that had cut me, the high school play I didn't make, the solo I didn't get, and the recognition that was given to someone else. It was as if every personal disappointment flooded my memory and added to the sorrow I felt for my son's experience.

When the sorrow eased, the unfounded anger came. Negative thoughts overtook common sense. *If that teacher doesn't think Josh is good enough for her top band, then he's not good enough for the lower band. Maybe I should pull him out of band all together.* I hurt because of my son's disappointment, and I wanted to protect Josh from being hurt again. No child of mine should ever experience disappointment! In my overly emotional state, I determined that the only way to avoid disappointment was to avoid trying.

In the midst of my mental tirade, God spoke to my heart and reminded me His Son had faced disappointment too, but that some things were worth persevering through. As I pondered this thought, I realized that Jesus had indeed faced many heartbreaking disappointments. He was discouraged when God's chosen people, the Jewish nation, didn't accept Him as the Messiah. He was disappointed when His closest friends didn't understand His teaching and even fell asleep during the darkest night of His life. He must have felt discouragement when a disciple betrayed Him, then another denied Him three times.

Jesus faced discouragement throughout His ministry here on earth—more than I will ever know. Yet, according to the Word of God, my eternal salvation was worth every disappointment Jesus faced. And in a gentle way, God urged me to learn how His Son reacted to disappointment and rejection.

With God's wisdom replacing a mom's emotions, I looked again at my son's situation. I knew this wouldn't be the last time he'd be disappointed, and I determined to help him (and me) work through it and learn from it. Although I'd love to shelter all my children from hurt, the truth is for children to succeed they need to learn to persevere when things don't turn out the way they hoped and when the result is worth the pain of trying again.

When our children face disappointment, there are four steps we can take to help them overcome.

Step One: Provide Unconditional Love

Disappointment comes from a number of different directions:

- We make a mistake and suffer the consequences.
- We try our best, but someone is better.
- Someone treats us unfairly.
- Circumstances are out of our control.

Regardless of the source, when a child is disappointed, the best gift we can give is unconditional love and support. Our children need to know in the depth of their hearts that their worth and value are *not* connected with their performance. We might be tempted to withhold affection or support if we think our child deserved to be disappointed. Maybe they didn't try as hard as they should have, or instead of practicing, they goofed off. However, all we have to do is look to the example given by our heavenly Father to know withholding unconditional love isn't a healthy or loving parenting practice. We often are disappointed because of our own sin, and yet God continues to love us and encourage us.

If a child scores low on a test because she didn't study, she still feels sad. Show your child you love her in spite of her shortcomings and that you believe in her. When God looks at us, He sees our potential and the brightness of our future. When we look at our child, we should see the same potential. Liberty Savard, in her book *Shattering Your Strongholds,* says this about God's plan for us: "Only with God can you start over more than once with an unblemished, untarnished,

100 percent, still-intact potential…the same potential He has always intended you to fulfill."[1]

When we look to Jesus for our example in this, we see Him clearly offering unconditional love to those whose sin was obvious and embraced, who turned their backs on Him, and those who disappointed Him most. This doesn't mean Jesus or we should affirm sin or negative and unhealthy choices, but we shouldn't punish a child by withholding love and faith in their ability to do better.

Step Two: Evaluate the Situation

As Jesus hung on the cross, He spoke these words of understanding, "Father, forgive them, for they do not know what they are doing" (Luke 23:34). Jesus saw the reason for the behavior of the Jewish people and His disciples. In the depth of His pain, He got to the root of His disappointment. When possible we should try to identify the reason for our child's disappointment and learn from it.

In high school I tried out for a vocal part in a play. During the audition they asked us to perform some dance moves. Although I had never danced before, I must have done something right because the director called me back to a second audition for dancing. Being clueless I went back to the next audition in heavy denim jeans and could barely lift my legs. Obviously I didn't get a part. To this day I wonder, *What was I thinking?* I wish I would have learned from that mistake and done a better job next time. Unfortunately I was so disappointed, I never tried out for another play, a vocal part, and definitely not a dancing role.

I should have evaluated my situation at that time. If I had, I might have come up with some better ways to handle the situation should it ever arise again. I would have learned to ask more questions of the director, made sure I understood what was expected, and talked to the other dancers. Then I would have been better equipped and left the straight-leg, button-fly 501 Levis at home.

Step Three: Check Your Attitude

Our children's attitude toward disappointment will shape the rest of their lives. They will learn to quit or persevere. They will learn unhealthy pride or humility. They will learn resentment or compassion.

Whether or not our kids have done their best, we can help them think through their reactions. My reaction to not making the play as a teenager was to quit trying. This was a mistake because I do have musical ability and often wish I had explored my potential. Some kids never explore their potential in a given area because they give up too soon. The truth is successful people fail just as much as other people—they *just don't quit*. Did you know that the best batters in baseball only get to first base 30 percent of the time? That means they fail 70 percent of the time!

When we face disappointments, quitting is one of the worst things we can do, but it's often the first thing we want to do. When we allow our children to quit because of one failure, we are missing the benefits God has nestled inside trials. Romans 5:3-4 says, "We also rejoice in our sufferings, because we know that suffering produces perseverance; perseverance, character; and character, hope." When we teach our children to try again, we collaborate with God to produce character in their lives and to implant hope in their hearts.

Other times we respond to disappointment with anger or blame. Parents say things like: "That coach is blind if he doesn't see my son's talent." "That teacher just picks her favorite." "They cheated." These responses teach children to allow anger to control their thoughts and speech and avoid accepting personal responsibility for their actions. Too many adults have grown up with a critical spirit, blaming others for missed opportunities.

To counteract these common responses, we can teach our children to do two things. The first is to take their thoughts captive to the obedience of Christ. As 2 Corinthians 10:5 admonishes, "We demolish arguments and every pretension that sets itself up against the knowledge of God, and we take captive every thought to make it obedient to Christ." Right thinking is a habit we can develop and learn at an early age. Children need to know they can control their thought life by choosing what they think about. They also learn that God desires us to submit all parts of our lives to Him, including our thoughts.

Once we submit our thought life to Christ, the second response is to speak only those words that build others up. Ephesians 4:29 says, "Do not let any unwholesome talk come out of your mouths, but only what is helpful for building others up according to their needs, that it may benefit those who listen." Discouragement is a breeding ground for angry, resentful words—about others or us. It starts in our minds and moves quickly to the lips. Once out of our mouths, discouraging words are like a brand on cattle—they sear lies into our heart.

Once I had my emotions in check, Josh and I discussed his feelings about not making Jazz I. We talked about how he should react to the boy who earned the bass spot. Josh decided to congratulate him sincerely. We discussed the teacher's offer to play bass in the lower band. Although he would be with younger students, he reasoned it would give him good practice. We were able to get past our emotions and talk about how to use a disappointing situation to live out the things we believe as Christians.

We chose to think affirming thoughts about all of the parties concerned and then speak positive words. It wasn't easy. It took a lot of discipline on my part to lead the discussion positively, but the results were worth meeting God's challenge to think and speak pleasingly.

Step Four: Plan Improvement

In almost every situation where a child is disappointed, there's an opportunity to improve. This might involve more study, private lessons, tutoring, working on social skills, extra practice at a sport, or concentrating on a character issue. As parents we have a limited number of years to help our children learn perseverance. Most kids don't know how to get from where they are to where they want to be. They need someone to teach them.

Josh had one more chance to make the top jazz band in eighth grade. Since my son loves music and has a God-given talent in this area, we decided to prepare him for that last chance. This took some strategic thinking and advance planning. Thankfully we had a complete year until the next auditions. The first thing we did was assess his chance at making the band by playing the bass guitar. We knew he'd be at a disadvantage again since his main competition would have a year of experience in the top band. However, no one played electric guitar in the top band. Since Josh wanted to play guitar anyway, he determined to learn a new instrument. With three years' experience playing bass, it wasn't a hard transition. To give him an added boost, we signed Josh up for private music lessons.

One year later Josh auditioned for Jazz I playing electric guitar. We waited another agonizing weekend and on Monday morning walked to the band room together. Another white envelope. Another silly grin. And another gut-wrenching moment took hold of me as Josh walked alone to read his personalized letter. But this year my son's face showed a different response. His sweet eyes peeked over the envelope, and his smile chased away all the fear in my heart. Josh had made the top jazz band!

While I can't guarantee that every one of Joshua's life disappointments will end the same way, I do know that he's much better prepared to overcome the next one. His mother is too.

Life is filled with little and big disappointments. Your child won't be invited to a party, she'll get cut from a team, and he may fail a test. The best training ground for dealing with disappointing situations is a loving home with parents who will respond with kindness, teach their children to learn from their mistakes, keep a God-pleasing attitude, and help their children dust themselves off when they fall and try harder next time.

Jesus is the best model we have for persevering through life's disappointments. In spite of the frustrations of dealing with human frailty, He chooses to love us, believe in us, and see our potential. When our children face disappointments, we can learn from Jesus and not give up.

Memory Verses

*We also rejoice in our sufferings, because we
know that suffering produces perseverance;
perseverance, character; and character, hope.*

ROMANS 5:3-4

*Do not let any unwholesome talk come out
of your mouths, but only what is helpful for
building others up according to their needs,
that it may benefit those who listen.*

EPHESIANS 4:29

*We demolish arguments and every pretension that sets
itself up against the knowledge of God, and we take
captive every thought to make it obedient to Christ.*

2 CORINTHIANS 10:5

I can do all things through Him who strengthens me.

PHILIPPIANS 4:13 NASB

*The LORD himself goes before you and will be
with you; he will never leave you nor forsake you.
Do not be afraid; do not be discouraged.*

DEUTERONOMY 31:8

*And now, dear brothers and sisters, one final thing.
Fix your thoughts on what is true, and honorable, and
right, and pure, and lovely, and admirable. Think
about things that are excellent and worthy of praise.*

PHILIPPIANS 4:8 NLT

Encouraging Words

*Success usually comes to those who are
too busy to be looking for it.*

—HENRY DAVID THOREAU

*Great works are performed not by
strength, but by perseverance.*

—SAMUEL JOHNSON

I am a slow walker, but I never walk backwards.

—ABRAHAM LINCOLN

To be happy, drop the words if only *and
substitute instead the words* next time.

—SMILEY BLANTON, M.D.

*It is not your aptitude, but your attitude,
that determines your altitude.*

—ZIG ZIGLAR

*Most of the important things in the world have
been accomplished by people who have kept on
trying when there seemed to be no hope at all.*

—DALE CARNEGIE

*Keep away from people who belittle your ambitions.
Small people always do that, but the really great
make you feel that you, too, can become great.*

—MARK TWAIN

It's always too soon to quit!

—NORMAN VINCENT PEALE

Discussion or Journal Questions

1. Identify a discouraging event that happened to you. What are some of the emotions you experienced as a result?

2. Read Joshua 1:1-9. This passage is written after the children of Israel had been wandering in the desert, looking for the promised land for 40 years. List some reasons why God would need to tell Joshua not to be discouraged.

3. What does God tell Joshua he needs to do to be "prosperous and successful"?

4. What are the promises God gives Joshua?

5. Read Hebrews 12:1. The author describes life as a race. What type of race does your life most resemble (examples: sprint, hurdle, relay, cross country, other)? Describe why.

6. As you seek to be obedient to God, what are some negative things that hinder you?

7. Even good things can hinder us from running the race laid out before us. Can you think of any examples in your life?

8. Read Hebrews 12:2-3. These verses tell us to "fix our eyes on Jesus." Why would watching Jesus help us in our challenges?

9. What helps you persevere when life gets tough?

10. Discouragement tends to hold us back by chaining us to our past. What does God say about our future in Jeremiah 29:11, Proverbs 23:17-19, Romans 8:37-39, and John 10:27-29?

Chapter Three

When Words Hurt

Sticks and stones may break my bones...

Y ou stole my sister!"

Thirty years later I can still remember the words, although the circumstances surrounding the accusation are fuzzy. Hands on her hips, she stood at my front door and demanded to have her sister returned. Obviously I didn't steal anyone. My friend was mad at me and annoyed that her sister was playing at my house. So she loaded her verbal arsenal and slung accusing words at me. They obviously stung, given the fact that I can still recall them now.

Growing up in a neighborhood of girls, I learned the power of words at an early age. Mostly we used words to encourage and have fun with each other. Every once in a while, however, we used mean words to manipulate and get our own way. It took longer to heal from those words than it did from the scrapes on our knees from roller-skating.

Words are powerful, and there is no denying that fact. God used words to speak the universe into being. "And God said, 'Let there be light'" (Genesis 1:3). He used words to call Moses into service. "This is what you are to say to the Israelites: 'I AM has sent me to you'" (Exodus 3:14). And He revealed Himself to humanity using a Word. "In the beginning was the Word, and the Word was with God, and the Word was God" (John 1:1). "The Word became flesh and made his dwelling among us" (John 1:14).

God created language as a way to communicate His love to creation—whispering words of love and correction through the prophets and writing love letters in the form of the Bible. How we have perverted this beautiful gift from God. Although words can communicate grand visions, they also communicate our displeasure. They have the power to build up a life or destroy it. A few unknowing teachers have shattered the dreams of youngsters in their classes. Thousands more have sparked flames of passion with a few aptly chosen words. Proverbs 15:23 (NLT) says, "Everyone enjoys a fitting reply; it is wonderful to say the right thing at the right time!"

Words have the power to influence the man or woman we will become. In her book *The Power of a Woman's Words*, Sharon Jaynes writes, "We are shaped by words from those who love us or refuse to love us. We are shaped by the words of those who don't even know our names. It is the heart cry of all mankind to be loved and accepted, and sometimes a simple word of encouragement can make all the difference."[1]

Words are more than a haphazard combination of 26 letters. Both direct and indirect messages flow from words. Everyone knows the falsity of the childhood saying, "Sticks and stones may break my bones, but words will never hurt me." Unless we build a brick wall around our hearts, words will hurt. However, with a healthy foundation and a discerning filter to process the words they hear, God will protect our children from damaging words.

Evaluate What You Hear

My undergraduate degree was in journalism with an emphasis on public relations, and reporting was an important element of my studies. In reporting we learned how to consider a topic from all angles and ask important questions to get to the truth. If the questions were solid, the answers would be interesting and strong. Weak questions produced a boring interview and an even more lackluster article. Because of my natural curiosity, I excelled at creating the questions. Today when learning anything new, I can exhaust the person sharing the information with questions. This skill has helped me process everything I hear, including unkind words.

Now when someone speaks words that are harsh, judgmental, or critical, I process those words through a series of questions. The answers help me determine how to respond.

Who?

The first question is, "Who spoke the words?" Is it someone close to you? Does that person love you? Does she have your best interest at heart? If the answer is yes, then we should listen more intently to the comments. Sometimes even those who love us can speak truth in inappropriate ways. If the person is a stranger, then it's easier to dismiss the comments as being judgmental.

What?

If you know the person who spoke the unkind words, then ask, "What is their character like?" Do they have a history of speaking the truth in love? Or do they have a history of lying, gossiping, or being critical? Do other people respect their opinion? If the person has a history of being critical, then you have just become another victim, and you should just move on. If their character is excellent, then pay more attention to the comment.

When?

If your child's teacher speaks unkindly at the end of a very difficult day, she does deserve more grace. This isn't making an excuse for bad behavior, but when you can identify that a normally kind person is under stress, it makes it easier to not take something personally. Also ask, "When did this person give godly counsel in the past?" If he has a history of sharing honest, loving rebuke, then the comment has more weight.

Why?

Ask, "Why would this person say this?" Is there an ulterior motive the person might have for speaking unkind words? Were they mad at the world and were you in the wrong place at the wrong time? Was it for their good or your good?

How?

A critical question we should all ask is, "How does this line up with Scripture?" If someone criticizes you for giving to the poor and tells you, "they'll just waste the money," you know they are speaking from a wrong heart. The Bible says, "He who gives to the poor will lack nothing, but he who closes his eyes to them receives many curses" (Proverbs 28:27). Jesus Himself said, "Go, sell everything you have and give to the poor, and you will have treasure in heaven. Then come, follow me" (Mark 10:21).

Also ask, "How would Jesus respond?" By using Jesus as our role model, we are assured of responding appropriately. This is why knowing Scripture is important to answering well.

~

Processing unkind words through a grid of questions helps to separate our emotions from fact. Too many people walk through life taking things personally and getting offended by passing comments. This is a painful way to live. Yes, people will say mean things, but we don't need to internalize those words. I find that taking a practical approach to words helps me decide which words I can ignore and which words could help.

Additionally, thinking the best of others is a habit and a choice. People who have been hurt in the past are justifiably suspicious. Helping your child choose to think the best of others is a discipline that will help him overcome many hurtful words.

Throughout their lives, our children will encounter people who use words to judge, criticize, shame, manipulate, blame, cause fear, and kill dreams. For the rest of this chapter, I'll share two examples of how words hurt and offer some responses to this specific type of pain.

Words That Judge and Criticize

Teaching our oldest son to drive was a learning experience—for him and me! In typical God fashion, the lessons weren't always about driving. Only God could take an average street corner and turn it into a life lesson that's now seared into my soul. Here's what happened on a not-so-average afternoon.

After taking short trips on side roads, I decided my son Josh was ready for the big time. So we headed to Costco one afternoon on a main thoroughfare. I don't normally drive at that time of the day, and I was unprepared for the amount of traffic. Josh was doing well until the light turned red just as he was pulling up to make a right turn. Because traffic was heavy, he was already driving slowly, but instead of stopping, I could tell Josh intended to keep going.

"Stop, Josh," I said quietly, as the car kept rolling.

"Stop, Josh," I said a little louder. The car kept moving, although it did slow down a bit. In a split second, I could tell Josh was going to turn right on a red, and I could see oncoming traffic starting to move. Why wasn't Josh stopping? I started to panic.

"Josh *stop!*" I yelled, and he slammed on the brakes.

"Mom, you're freaking me out," Josh gasped.

"Josh, you're freaking *me* out!" I answered, as we both sat there in shock. Josh explained that he thought I meant for him to slow down when I said "stop." I didn't have time to sort out his thought process on that one because just then the light turned green, and Josh turned right...legally and safely.

I told Josh I was sorry for yelling at him. He said he was sorry he didn't listen to me, and we were back on good ground. At least I thought so. Seconds later a young guy who had been behind us when Josh slammed on the breaks pulled up on our left and motioned for us to roll down the window. Thinking there was something wrong with a tire, Josh rolled down his window. The guy said, "Hey, if you are going to act like that, take your sticker off your car." Then he sped off.

The incident rattled Josh and made me mad. I knew he was talking about our church window decal, and I alternated between anger at his judgmental attitude and shame that someone might think badly about God because of a driving incident. Honestly, anger was the predominate emotion. I couldn't stand that someone would judge my son or me without knowing anything about us.

We both stewed over this incident for weeks. Josh didn't want to get behind the wheel for a while, and I had to deal with my unkind thoughts toward that young man who judged us. Finally I had to deal with the truth—people judge us all the time. They judge us based on our looks, the cars we drive, the clothes we wear, and the words we speak. They will also judge us on the mistakes we make, especially if they know we are Christians. As Christians we are targeted. People will be looking for ways to point out our failures or inconsistencies, and it will hurt.

Jesus spoke these words to His followers, "Do not judge, or you too will be judged. For in the same way you judge others, you will be judged, and with the measure you use, it will be measured to you" (Matthew 7:1-2). Josh and I definitely experienced being judged, and it wasn't pleasant.

Knowing that Jesus was also judged and criticized unfairly brings me comfort when it happens to me. Jesus was perfect, yet people found fault with Him then and now. Judgment of this kind occurs when two things happen—when someone only has partial knowledge of you and they add their own expectations on top of that incomplete knowledge. People didn't always take the time to know Jesus, but they sure knew what they wanted Him to do.

In response to the judgment, Jesus made *not one* change to who He was or His mission. He did not change His approach to ministry. He did not soften His teaching. He did not stop healing on the Sabbath. He did not stop touching the "unclean." Jesus knew His mission and revealed it in Luke 19:10, "For the Son of Man came to seek and to save what was lost." He was fully committed to the task His Father gave Him.

When people judge or criticize our children or us, we can follow the footsteps of Jesus and stay committed to who we are and our calling. The best advice we can give our children is to not make a change based on other people's expectations. If they do, they will forever be adapting who they are and what God has called them to do based on someone else's thoughts.

When that other driver criticized Josh and me, the first thing I wanted to do was remove the church sticker from my car window. I never wanted that type of attack again! However, that would have been giving in. I put that sticker on my car for a reason, and I left it there.

The judgment of others always threatens to sidetrack us. It consumes mental energy to sort through the emotions. However, the Bible encourages us to fix our eyes on Jesus when someone finds fault with us.

Hebrews 12:1-3 offers us words of encouragement that we all should commit to memory:

> Therefore, since we are surrounded by such a great cloud of witnesses, let us throw off everything that hinders and the sin that so easily entangles, and let us run with perseverance the race marked out for us. Let us fix our eyes on Jesus, the author and perfecter of our faith, who for the joy set before him endured the cross, scorning its shame, and sat down at the right hand of the throne of God. Consider him who endured such opposition from sinful men, so that you will not grow weary and lose heart.

Words That Shame

The football coach made a point to say he would never use shaming words on the field. Yet on the first night of practice, one of the assistant coaches yelled at the boys, "Ladies! Get moving!"

The field of junior high boys leapt into action, while I wanted to leap onto the field myself only for a different reason. Apparently that adult used the demeaning words to motivate those boys. While they may have resulted in short-term results, those words have the potential to inflict long-term damage on the hearts of those children.

I'll never forget the words of my history teacher at Alhambra High School years ago. When I was a junior, I asked to meet a teacher after school to discuss the results of the first test of the year.

I earned a C and wanted to know how to study better for the next test. She sat at her desk as I asked for help, tilted her chin down, and looked at me over her reading glasses saying, "You aren't an A student, are you?"

I can think of plenty of answers now, but back then I was an awkward 16-year-old, who probably mumbled a few words and got out of there as fast as possible. Indignity rises up in my chest just thinking about that experience. No adult should shame a child—but it happens all the time.

Demeaning words often place some form of guilt on a child—to suggest that somehow the situation is her fault. The football coach didn't like what the boys were doing, so he spewed out the worst name to call a young boy. My teacher obviously thought I deserved a C and couldn't do better. This is a lazy, unkind way to approach correction.

When our children face words that demean, there are two important things to do. First, stand on the Word of God, which says no one can condemn them. Romans 8:1 claims, "Therefore, there is now no condemnation for those who are in Christ Jesus." Jesus Christ took on every one of our sins, so that we could stand pure in front of God. No one can pass on guilt to us or our children.

Secondly, instead of allowing words to defeat us, these words can spur us on to do better. Someone has already spoken the words, so there's nothing we can do about them. However, we determine their effect on us from that point on. I'll admit that the history teacher's words made me mad. Even then I knew it was wrong for her to speak to me in that way. I already knew I needed to improve. Instead of giving up, her words sparked a flame to prove her wrong—not because I wanted to earn her approval, but because I wanted to improve myself.

We cannot control what others say or do. We can only control ourselves. By turning a negative comment into a challenge, our children develop the inner discipline to press on despite the disparaging words of others.

How to Respond

When someone has wronged us, the greater danger is to return another wrong, either in thought or in deed. Many people who are sinned against are completely innocent until they choose to retaliate—then they are just as guilty as the offending party.

Guard Your Thoughts and Words

When someone wrongs us verbally, it is human nature to want to hurt them back. First, we do this in our mind. Then we speak unkind words directly back to the offender or by gossiping about the person to a compassionate friend. Neither one is a godly response. Ecclesiastes 10:20 says, "Do not revile the king even in your thoughts, or curse the rich in your bedroom, because a bird of the air may carry your words, and a bird on the wing may report what you say."

We often misinterpret the words of Jesus and practice doing unto others as they have done unto us. However, Jesus said something strikingly different. He said, "Do to others as you would have them do to you" (Luke 6:31). By learning to guard their thoughts and behavior, our children can avoid more heartache because of their own sin.

Use the Comments to Improve Yourself

One of God's greatest blessings to us is His ability to bring good out of evil. That means even though we are experiencing a difficult and painful time, God is already working behind the scenes to cause a blessing for those who love Him. When words hurt our children, their first response will probably not be to see the good in it. As parents we can help train our children to expect God's good—because it will come. One way to seek the good is to be open to truth hidden within the inappropriately voiced words.

To see truth takes a humble heart. That's challenging at best when everything in us screams like a cheerleader on a football field, "Defense!" Rabbi Joseph Telushkin has studied the impact of words and makes this observation about our response to them.

When criticized, many of us deny or minimize the faults being pointed out; we blame somebody else, perhaps even the critic, or insist, both to the person offering the criticism and ourselves that we cannot change.[2]

We miss a powerful opportunity to improve ourselves when that happens. Telushkin acknowledges that we need to ignore some people, especially when criticism is all they offer. However, with others we should listen to their words with an open heart. Telushkin continues:

Of course, there's a good chance that the person criticizing us has numerous faults; indeed she even might be guilty of the very flaw that she is pointing out in you. But unless we have reason to believe that her real goal is to undermine our sense of self-worth, we should quash such thoughts as *What gives her the right to criticize me? Look at her flaws.* Instead, we should ask: "Is what she is saying true?" Even if the critic's point is exaggerated, that is no excuse to reject everything she has said. Instead, we should ask: "Is there some validity in the criticism? Can I take what she has said, and use it to improve myself?" Only someone who is already perfect doesn't need to learn to accept criticism, but such a person does not exist.[3]

Learn to Forgive

Learning to forgive is an important part of dealing with unkind words. Many adults grow up with unforgiveness doing more damage in their hearts than the original offense. Jesus was very clear on the importance of forgiveness. In Matthew 6:14, Jesus said, "For if you forgive men when they sin against you, your heavenly Father will also forgive you." Did you notice the condition required for receiving God's forgiveness? That we forgive others.

Forgiveness is a complicated process that takes even mature adults years to learn. Often we need to forgive someone repeatedly until the pain they caused has lessened over time. To help your child rid his heart of unforgiveness, consider praying together. Although your child may not *feel* like forgiving the person who hurt her, she can *choose* to forgive. Through this process God will honor her desire to forgive and bring increased healing over the hurtful words.

When a Parent's Words Hurt

Cheri Nace is a devoted mother, committed to raising her children in a godly fashion. Like most parents, Cheri experiences frustration with her children. And like most parents, at times that frustration reveals itself through impatient words and tones. Cheri knew God wanted her to deal with this, but she felt discouraged with herself and the challenge of change.

One day she read a Scripture that profoundly impacted her. It was Proverbs 18:21: "The tongue has the power of life and death, and those who love it will eat its fruit." Here's what happened in Cheri's own words.

> This afternoon, as I was visiting the blogs I usually read on a daily basis, what God has been trying to tell me *finally* hit me smack in the face. I have obviously heard Him a thousand times before but for some reason just never listened—maybe because it was going to be too much work to change.
>
> This is what got me. "The tongue has the power of life and death, and those who love it will eat its fruit" (Proverbs 18:21).
>
> Wow! The things I say have the power of life and death, the power to crush a spirit or to raise it up. I was stunned by the profound truth of those words. Sometimes in the rush of my morning, I don't always send my kids off to school with their spirits filled with love. They are crushed. I noticed it this morning in my son's face as I yelled at him to hurry up. Get your shoes and socks on *now*! The sparkle went out of his eyes.
>
> My heart hurt for him. So I tried my best before that bus came to regain some sort of happiness for him so he wouldn't climb

on the bus feeling dejected. I asked him if there was anything going on at school today that he was looking forward to. His eyes lit up as he said, "Yeah, my teacher is going to read a Junie B. Jones book about Valentine's Day!" I thanked the Lord for correcting me in time to repair the morning.

When I look back at all the times I have sent them off to school feeling sad and lonely because of my words, it tears me up. What power words have! *The power of life and death.*

There is another verse that keeps my words in check. Psalm 19:14 says, "May the words of my mouth and the meditation of my heart be pleasing in your sight." I now have these two verses taped everywhere in my house. They are on my bathroom mirror, the hood of my stove, the fireplace mantel, the banister of the stairs, and even on the tank of the toilet!

I sure can relate with Cheri's frustration. There have been far too many times when I should have responded better to a child—times when I wish my tone of voice and words had been laced with patience and kindness rather than unjustified anger. I have spoken words that left my children sad and me wishing I could press the rewind button and keep my mouth zipped.

Unfortunately I often respond better to the bigger challenges of parenting than the everyday frustrations. If you were a fly on my kitchen wall for a day, you would wonder why a minor event sparked such an annoyed response. If your house is like mine, the answer is because that minor event you saw happen once actually happens frequently. Hence, I fall into the if-I've-told-you-once-I've-told-you-a-thousand-times trap of thinking, which doesn't lend itself to much mercy.

When my patience wears thin, I find myself strikingly similar to the person spoken about in Ecclesiastes 7:9: "Do not be quickly provoked in your spirit, for anger resides in the lap of fools." Ouch! I sure don't want to be a fool with a lap of anger. Because when that lap is full, it only takes the slightest spark for frustration and anger to spill over onto some unsuspecting victims.

I've never done anything as difficult as being a mother. While the first part of motherhood—the physical part—was tough, it was incomparable to the rest of it.

There's this ideal mother I want to be, and then there's…well…me. Disappointing at times. Frustrated at my inability to snap my fingers and change. I completely understand why my children look at me when I ask them why they did what they did and say, "I don't know." I get what Paul said in Romans 7:15: "I do not understand what I do. For what I want to do I do not do, but what I hate I do."

God is calling me to deal with frustration that leads to unkind words in a healthy and godly way. I've found a three-step process is in order when I've messed up. First, I ask forgiveness from my child. This sometimes takes getting down on my knees literally, looking my child in the face, and saying, "I'm very sorry. I was wrong." Second, I ask forgiveness from God. If I just go on as if nothing has happened, there is no opportunity for God's healing to occur in my heart. I must address ongoing parental frustration as a spiritual issue and bring my concerns to God in prayer. I find confessing my sin opens the door for God to bring His healing peace into my heart. When I don't confess inappropriate anger and words to God, it just starts building up—making me a fool with a full lap. Third, I need to accept God's forgiveness and grace. I'm so glad God offers me forgiveness when I mess up and puts me back on the path of developing a sweet spirit of patience and gentleness. That's the kind of mother I want to be.

The Bible has very good news for me when I think I'll never change, that I'm too weak, and need more self-discipline but don't know how to get it. The words of Jesus, recorded by the apostle Paul, bring me hope: "But he said to me, 'My grace is sufficient for you, for my power is made perfect in weakness.' Therefore I will boast all the more gladly about my weaknesses, so that Christ's power may rest on me" (2 Corinthians 12:9).

That's good news for me because there are times as a mother I sure feel weak. Being a parent is hard work. I'm so glad God has given me grace.

The Power of a Parent's Words

Our children need to hear significantly more positive words to offset the negative ones they will hear throughout the day. Each loving, kind word we speak is a blessing that fills up their emotional bank account, in preparation for the inevitable withdrawal due to unkind words. This need for children to receive a verbal blessing from their parents goes back to the Old Testament. Back then parents reserved a blessing for a special occasion. Today we can apply the formula for blessing our children every day.

Gary Smalley and John Trent, both family counselors, wrote about this concept in their book *The Blessing*. While there were unique aspects to an Old Testament blessing, they identified five powerful relationship elements parents can use today:

- Meaningful touch
- A spoken message
- Attaching "high value" to the one being blessed
- Picturing a special future for the one being blessed
- An active commitment to fulfill the blessing[4]

Blessing our children can be done informally, by placing a hand on a shoulder and expressing the child's value to you. We might express confidence in their ability to complete a task in the future—such as doing well on a test or finishing high school. We might even share our hopes for their success in the future and our belief in their ability to fulfill that hope.

The New Testament speaks of the importance of blessing others and the promise of being blessed as a result. Although this verse doesn't speak directly to parents and children, many households might long for the harmony mentioned.

> Finally, all of you, live in harmony with one another; be sympathetic, love as brothers, be compassionate and humble. Do not repay evil with evil or insult with insult, but with blessing,

because to this you were called so that you may inherit a blessing. For, "Whoever would love life and see good days must keep his tongue from evil and his lips from deceitful speech" (1 Peter 3:8-10).

Using our words to build up rather than tear down can impact our children's lives forever. Loving words have a powerful ripple effect. It really doesn't take much to affirm our children's value. Sometimes it just takes a few words, as in this story told by Mary Ann Bird in *The Whisper Test.*

> I grew up knowing I was different, and I hated it. I was born with a cleft palate, and when I started school, my classmates made it clear to me how I looked to others: a little girl with a misshapen lip, crooked nose, lopsided teeth, and garbled speech. When schoolmates asked, "What happened to your lip?" I'd tell them I'd fallen and cut it on a piece of glass. Somehow it seemed more acceptable to have suffered an accident than to have been born different. I was convinced that no one outside my family could love me. There was, however, a teacher in the second grade whom we all adored—Mrs. Leonard by name. She was short, round, happy—a sparkling lady. Annually we had a hearing test. Mrs. Leonard gave the test to everyone in the class, and finally it was my turn. I knew from past years that as we stood against the door and covered one ear, the teacher sitting at her desk would whisper something, and we would have to repeat it back—things like "The sky is blue" or "Do you have new shoes?" I waited there for those words that God must have put into her mouth, those seven words that changed my life. Mrs. Leonard said, in her whisper, "I wish you were my little girl."[5]

As parents we can give our children the gift of unconditional love expressed through words. In doing so, may we point them to the Author of words, the Giver of life.

Memory Verses

*Keep reminding them of these things. Warn them
before God against quarreling about words; it is
of no value, and only ruins those who listen.*

2 TIMOTHY 2:14

*An anxious heart weighs a man down,
but a kind word cheers him up.*

PROVERBS 12:25

*Why do you look at the speck of sawdust in your
brother's eye and pay no attention to the plank in your
own eye? How can you say to your brother, "Let me
take the speck out of your eye," when all the time there
is a plank in your own eye? You hypocrite, first take
the plank out of your own eye, and then you will see
clearly to remove the speck from your brother's eye.*

MATTHEW 7:3-5

*They overcame him by the blood of the Lamb and
by the word of their testimony; they did not love
their lives so much as to shrink from death.*

REVELATION 12:11

*May the words of my mouth and the meditation
of my heart be pleasing in your sight, O
LORD, my Rock and my Redeemer.*

PSALM 19:14

*All kinds of animals, birds, reptiles and creatures
of the sea are being tamed and have been tamed
by man, but no man can tame the tongue.
It is a restless evil, full of deadly poison.*

JAMES 3:7-8

Encouraging Words

*Fools live to regret their words, wise
men to regret their silence.*

—WILLIAM HENRY

*No one has a prosperity so high and firm that
two or three words can't dishearten it.*

—RALPH WALDO EMERSON

*The difference between the right word
and the almost right word is the difference
between lightning and a lightning bug.*

—MARK TWAIN

*Kind words are short and easy to speak,
but their echoes are truly endless.*

—MOTHER TERESA

*Man does not live by words alone, despite the
fact that sometimes he has to eat them.*

—ADLAI STEVENSON

Discussion or Journal Questions

1. Can you remember words that changed your life for good or bad? What were those words and how did they impact you?

2. Read James 3:7-8. Why are our words (the tongue) so difficult for us to control?

3. In what ways do we use our tongue to dishonor others or God?

4. Do you have a successful way to process hurtful words? Describe your response.

5. How can you tell if your thoughts are judgmental or helpful?

6. What are some ways to guard our hearts and minds from being judgmental?

7. Read Matthew 7:3-5. How does taking the "plank" out of our eyes help us see clearly?

8. Why is it so easy to speak unkind words to someone in our own family?

9. What practices can you implement to control your tongue? Write these down and review them often.

10. Identify ways you can verbally bless your children this week.

Chapter Four

Overcoming Fear

Along came a spider who sat down beside her...

Standing in front of my sixth-grade classroom, ready to recite a poem I'd memorized, my heart pounded. Was it "Beware the Jabberwock, I said" or "Beware the Jabberwock, my son"? "The jaws that bite" or "The jaws that might"? Oh my goodness, I was scared. Fear jumbled the words in my mind. If I messed up, not only would I get a lower grade, but the entire class would witness my humiliation.

Fear has to be one of the worst emotions we experience. It rips confidence from under our feet, makes knees buckle, and hands shake. Whether it's joining a new Sunday-school class, taking a test, facing a bully, or walking into a dark room, almost every child deals with fear. Fear certainly wasn't part of God's original design for His creation. In the Garden of Eden, God created the earth to be a place where there was nothing to fear because everything was under Adam's control (Genesis 1:28-29). Unfortunately, due to disobedience and sin on the part of Adam and Eve, all that changed in a bite.

After Adam and Eve ate from the one tree in the Garden God told them not to eat from, we have the first recorded incident of fear. Adam and Eve knew they had done wrong. In fact their disobedience led to an awareness of their naked condition, and they hid from God. But God didn't let them stay hidden. He called to them, and Adam replied, "I heard you in the garden, and I was afraid because I was naked; so I hid" (Genesis 3:10).

Their sin and subsequent fear led to a division in the perfect relationship God had with Adam and Eve. God didn't want them to be afraid, and He doesn't want us to be afraid. Unfortunately fear seems to be an increasingly common condition among children, taking a variety of forms.

Depending on the severity of the fear, a child can experience mild physical sensations, such as an upset tummy, to a more severe reaction, which might cause them to withdraw from others. You probably know these symptoms well, as most of us remember our childhood fears with crystal clarity. One of my most vivid memories happened in the summer before fifth grade.

In my elementary school, the campus was divided between the lower and upper grades. First through fourth composed the lower grades, and fifth through eighth the upper. Not only was there a geographic difference, but the upper grades had a separate playground, rotated between classes, and ate a later lunch. As the start of fifth grade approached, my anxiety level increased.

Everything about fifth grade scared me. How would I wait another hour to eat? What would it be like being with all the big kids? Could I handle the homework? I was a wreck. On the first day of school, I was so sick with fear, I ended up in the nurse's office.

One day later I was fine. All those unknowns of fifth grade became known, and I was no longer a quivering mess. Experts say that some children are more prone to fear, and I was one of those. It would be nice to announce that I outgrew the tendency to fall apart in the face of fear, but I haven't. This uniquely qualifies me to write this chapter, as I have spent a lifetime dealing with fear and learning how to overcome what could debilitate me.

Healthy Versus Unhealthy Fear

God did create us with two types of healthy and natural fear. The first is one of God's ways of protecting us from harm, and we might describe it more accurately as caution. A child learns to keep his fingers away from a hot stove because it will hurt him, and that fear keeps the child safe. That same boy learns that diving into a pond headfirst is dangerous, and the fear of being paralyzed prompts him to jump in feet first. As adults we learn that driving too fast is risky and expensive, and the fear of hurting others and our pocketbook reminds us to *not* put the pedal to the metal.

Parents should teach and encourage healthy caution. We want our children to have a good sense of danger and make wise and safe choices because there are real dangers in our world.

The other healthy fear is the fear of God. This is not a fear that drives us from God but allows us to approach Him with a healthy awe and respect. Deuteronomy 6:13 records this advice in the Old Testament: "Fear the LORD your God, serve him only." The apostle Luke records this testimony of a healthy fear of God in the early years of the church: "Then the church throughout Judea, Galilee and Samaria enjoyed a time of peace. It was strengthened; and encouraged by the Holy Spirit, it grew in numbers, living in the fear of the Lord" (Acts 9:31).

Healthy fears drive us to make good decisions, while unhealthy fears do the opposite. If left unaddressed, unhealthy fears cause us to distort the balance in our lives—we end up pulling away from one fear and twisting sideways to avoid another.

I believe God longs to raise up generation after generation of bold and courageous followers. Unfortunately just the opposite seems to be happening. So many of us intentionally avoid situations where we know we'll be afraid, causing us to create safe lives where we aren't tested or pushed out of our comfort zones.

We are passing these benign lives down to our children, who will live behind their own sets of brick fences, only occasionally daring to risk something for God. Fear is one of the greatest hindrances to obedience, hence it is eternally important that we help our children deal with it.

Identify Common Fears

There are certain common fears that manifest themselves more at given ages. For example, many babies and toddlers face separation anxiety when taken from one parent or the other. Children between the ages of four and six often are afraid of things that aren't based in reality, such as monsters. Children who are seven and above most often deal with fears that are based in reality, such as injuries to themselves or others or natural disasters, such as earthquakes and tornados.

Whether the source is real or imagined, fear is fear. Our children's bodies, hearts, and minds react in much the same way. As parents we can help our children deal with all of these common fears.

All children will experience fear at one time or another, and this fear tends to be directed at a specific object, individual, or circumstance. However, when fear covers your child like a blanket, and she experiences high anxiety with no specific threat or cause in view, there might be more to it than normal childhood issues. Some children may develop fears that need to be addressed by a professional.

In the last chapter of this book, I have explained how to know when your child's fears are outside of normal fears. If you have any concerns about this issue, please seek professional help.

Create a Culture of Openness

Children need to know it is okay to express fear. One of the most detrimental things we can do to a child is to label her fears as unimportant or belittle her for feeling afraid. Making jokes or trying to tease a child out of a fear doesn't work. Not only is the child still afraid, but she adds embarrassment over the fear to her list of worries. This is one of Satan's greatest tools to harm our emotional health and keep us ineffective for God.

To raise children who will deal with fear head-on and develop into courageous adults, we must start with exactly where they are. Hidden fear only festers and grows. We must open up to the truth for healing to come. We can help our children move from fear to faith by allowing them to express fears in a safe and nonjudgmental setting.

This culture of openness will become critically important if your child ever faces a dangerous situation outside of your care. This happened in our home a few years ago after I allowed another parent to drive two of my children to a birthday party. After the party, one of my kids came home with an unsettled look on his face. It took a while to pull it out of him. The neighbor had driven to the party while drinking a can of beer. My son was afraid during the entire party and didn't know what to do. Thankfully no one was injured, and I was glad he could share his fear with me. It was a painful learning experience for all of us.

Sadly our children do face real dangers outside of our care. We can encourage our children's natural intuition by allowing them to express even the initial hint of fear in a new setting. Always take your child's fear of a caregiver seriously. Then, as a parent, you can thoroughly research the situation to determine what's really going on.

This verbalization of fear might not be an easy task, as it is often difficult to identify the true source of anxiety. Helping a child put fears into words takes time, patience, and creativity. It may help for a parent to share memories of when they were young and afraid. Stories of other people's fears are reassuring as well—it's best to first get permission when sharing about other people's experiences. We all want to know we aren't the only ones who are afraid.

Author William Sears, in his article "7 Ways to Help Your Child Handle Fear," offers this advice. "Without reinforcing your child's fears, empathize with them: 'When I was a child, I was afraid of a dark bedroom, too.' Acknowledge your child's fears in order to help her work through them. Strike a balance. Don't ignore the fears, but don't get over-involved in them either, or your child will play up the fear to get your attention."[1]

It's important to verbalize fear to someone because Satan tries to use it to isolate us from others. By becoming aware of our own emotions, we can submit our fears and weaknesses to God instead of locking them inside. This opens the door for Him to work in the situation and in our hearts.

Desensitize Your Child

Depending on the type of fear, it may help your child to expose him gradually to the source of that fear. For example, a child who is afraid of starting kindergarten may benefit from several weeks of "practice." This might involve getting up a bit earlier each day, packing a backpack, picking out clothes, or learning how to put the straw in a juice box by himself. Then practice walking to school, finding the classroom, and figuring out the locations of the bathrooms. Most children have a hard time putting their exact fears into words. By walking through all scenarios of a fearful situation, you may be able to uncover something hidden.

Because childhood is full of scary "firsts," this practice can be very helpful for years to come. Unless you have a naturally bold and adventurous child (only one out of our five children fit this description), you will have the opportunity to help your child overcome many first-time fears. This could include a move, dealing with animals, sleeping alone in a dark room, a trip to the dentist, the first trip to camp, puberty changes, trying out for a sports team, or even going to a new church.

By gradually exposing your child to a new situation, she will address her fears within the safety of your presence. Physically walk through the new circumstances together beforehand when possible. If that's not possible, then verbally walk through it. Try to incorporate every detail, even those that seem minor to you. As a fearful child myself, it was often the little things I worried most about.

For preverbal children the same gradual exposure plan can work. Because most early fears involve separation, start by only being gone a short time and gradually increase it as necessary. Your child will learn that you will return, and he or she will learn coping skills at an early age.

What doesn't work well with first-time fears is rationalization. Telling your child that nine out of ten kids will not wet their pants in first grade isn't very helpful because if your child is like me, I'm convinced I will be the one kid it will happen to. Statistics still don't work for me. But by helping your child walk through the situation—either physically or verbally—you can deal head-on with the unknown and alleviate a lot of worry.

Have an Action Plan

Having an action plan does not mean giving your child a cell phone and having him call you if he wants to come home—unless, of course, something dangerous is happening. Our goal in this chapter is to help children develop their own ways to handle and overcome fear, while not relying on Mom or Dad all the time. Having a plan of action for fearful situations is another tool that can help.

Playing the "What If?" game can be very beneficial for uncovering fears and giving your child a sense of control. Together identify every fearful possibility and a course of action. *What if you are at a sleepover and they start telling ghost stories? What if you are at school and you think you are going to throw up? What if you try out for baseball and get hit on the head with the ball? What if you go to a dance and no one asks you to dance?*

Just bringing the fear into the light weakens its power. By adding a problem-solving component, you are equipping your child to be proactive.

In their book *Your Anxious Child*, authors John Dacey and Lisa Fiore offer a fantastic way to deal with fears in an activity they call "I Guess It's Not So Scary After All." In this activity, they suggest sitting down with your child and making a list of every reason for anxiety. List them one by one on the left side of a piece of paper. Then the authors suggest the following approach. "Go through the list, and for each negative, frightening consequence that your child mentions, change it into a positive, exciting one. For example, 'What if the other kids don't like me?' can be changed to 'What if I make good friends?'"[2]

This activity teaches your child to change her thinking from negative to positive and to see things in a different light.

Don't Let Fear Win

While some fear is certainly a God-given protective instinct, other fear actually can keep your child from doing the right thing. It's in these situations we need to grit our teeth and encourage our children to move past the fear and do it anyway.

I teach quite a bit at my home church, and at an event-planning meeting once, a fellow church member asked me if I get nervous before I speak. I answered, "No, I'm not nervous here." Another woman responded by saying, "That's how you can tell you are in God's will, if you don't have any fear."

I didn't want to correct her in front of those people, but I couldn't disagree more. God's people have always felt fear, and I do in other speaking settings. In the Bible there are almost 200 references to people being afraid. In the New Revised Standard version there are 66 verses where the exact words "do not be afraid" are used. Here are some examples:

- God told Abraham, "Do not be afraid."
- God told Isaac, "Do not be afraid."
- God told Jacob, "Do not be afraid."
- God told Moses, "Do not be afraid."
- God told Joshua, "Do not be afraid."

I could go on. Why do you think God had to tell the heroes of our faith not to be afraid? It's because they were *afraid*! They weren't *feeling* confident, strong, or courageous when they set out to obey God. They were *feeling* fear.

John Ortberg makes this observation in *If You Want to Walk on Water, You've Got to Get Out of the Boat*, "My hunch is the reason God says 'Fear not' so much is not that he wants us to be spared emotional discomfort. In fact, usually he says it to get people to do something that is going to lead them into greater fear anyway. I think God says 'fear not' so often because fear is the number one reason human beings are tempted to avoid doing what God asks them to do."[3]

Here's the truth about those heroes of our faith, those mighty men and women who saw God perform miracles. They didn't let fear stop them! They took the first step of obedience in the midst of their fears.

The Bible also includes examples of times when fear did stop the people of God from being obedient. I love God's response in one situation. It's not what I would have expected, but it gives me a picture of God's true heart toward dealing with us when fear stops us from doing the right thing.

Exodus 14 tells of the Israelites' escape from the Egyptian army. As the Israelites get to the edge of the sea, with over 600 chariots on their heels, they complain to Moses and cry out to God in terror. They are so afraid of the future that they express a desire to be back in slavery in Egypt. Here's what the Scripture says:

> As Pharaoh approached, the Israelites looked up, and there were the Egyptians, marching after them. They were terrified and cried out to the LORD. They said to Moses, "Was it because there were no graves in Egypt that you brought us to the desert to die? What have you done to us by bringing us out of Egypt? Didn't we say to you in Egypt, 'Leave us alone; let us serve the Egyptians'? It would have been better for us to serve the Egyptians than to die in the desert!" (Exodus 14:10-12).

Moses is a gentle and compassionate leader in that moment, and he reminds the people of God's faithfulness.

> Moses answered the people, "Do not be afraid. Stand firm and you will see the deliverance the LORD will bring you today. The Egyptians you see today you will never see again. The LORD will fight for you; you need only to be still" (Exodus 14:13-14).

I love Moses' patient and encouraging response. He's kind of like a sweet grandpa. He acknowledges the people's fears and actually agrees with them to not take the next step but to stand firm. God's answer in this particular situation is a bit different: "Then the LORD said to Moses, 'Why are you crying out to me? Tell the Israelites to move on'" (Exodus 14:15).

To sum up the situation, the Israelites are following God's leading to a promised land, they've seen him perform miracles to set them free, and they stand there complaining, frozen in fear and resigned to die. All the while God is waiting for them to *move!*

I've found that sometimes God waits for us to make the first move in the midst of our fears. My parental instinct in this regard isn't always the best for my children. If it were up to me, I would protect them from every potentially frightening situation. But in doing so, I am teaching them to let fear stop them.

Dealing with a child's fear starts when they are babies. Babies are often resistant to new people. What mom wants her sweet little baby to cry when left in the church nursery? So that caring mom decides she'll keep her baby with her. When baby is a toddler, he hasn't learned that the loving volunteers in the church nursery are safe, so he continues to cry in fear every Sunday morning. What's a loving mom to do? So she fosters the fear and takes junior with her. Do you see the pattern developing?

I'm so thankful my husband has a better sense of dealing with fear than I. That's why my kids will ride roller coasters, jump off high dives, and climb mountains. If it were up to me, we would all stay glued to the ground. But if that happened, my children would never go on mission trips, serve the homeless on the streets, minister in prisons, or reach out to drug addicts. In other words my fears could keep them from doing the very work Jesus calls them to do—the dirty, risky, and potentially dangerous stuff of ministry.

Do Not Rescue

When your child has gathered his courage and done something in spite of his fear, do not rescue him in the middle of the act. When I went to the nurse's office in fifth grade, my mother did not come and pick me up. There was compassion, but there was no rescue. After a time in the office, I returned to my class.

Parents, especially moms, need to do whatever it takes to hide their own concern for their child's fear. This might mean pasting on a big smile and waving goodbye until junior's bus has rounded the corner on its way to school. Then you can go collapse in tears and call a friend for support. Just don't let your child see it, or it will feed his fears.

Words of Affirmation

When a child has faced her fears and stepped out to do something with knees shaking and heart pounding, that is something worth acknowledging and celebrating. Take a moment to affirm your child's bravery with words of affirmation.

- I'm proud of you! You were afraid, and you did it anyway.
- That was very brave.
- You are becoming very courageous.

It is crucial that we build our children's confidence, especially in areas of fear. Many adults remember with shame and sorrow the time that fear stopped them from doing something important and brave. By affirming your child's choices, it's like adding cement to the building block of their character development.

Teach Your Child to Trust God Above All Else

Psalm 20:7 says, "Some trust in chariots and some in horses, but we trust in the name of the LORD our God." Although the psalmist wrote those words thousands of years ago, I wonder if this generation underestimates God's capabilities and trusts in its own "horses" and "chariots." We may have a head knowledge about trusting God, but in reality we trust in a company for our financial security or our physical strength for our safety.

Unfortunately we can unknowingly pass this lack of trust on to our children by our actions and words. Children are always watching and learning from our example. They learn not to trust God with their money when we don't tithe. They learn not to risk big things for God when they watch us playing it safe. They learn to worry when they watch us pace and fret.

What we can teach our children is we serve a God who is big enough and powerful enough to answer our prayers, to meet our daily needs, to intervene in our lives for our good, and to work miracles on our behalf. We do this by showing our children that *we* turn to God in times of need and then sharing how God answered that need.

Prayer is our primary opportunity for teaching children about the faithfulness of God. Children don't need to know all the details of a problem. But when we wisely and carefully pray with our children about our needs, they get to witness God in action. They learn for themselves that God can be trusted. As John Ortberg writes, "Trust and fear have been battling each other for the human heart—your heart—a long time now. Eventually one or the other will win."[4] Parents have the divine opportunity to sow prayer into their children's hearts, preparing them for a harvest of faith.

What Will Your Children Do for God?

Because I have dealt with the issue of fear for many years, I sometimes teach on the subject and start with this question, "If you could do anything for God, and know you wouldn't fail, what would you do?"

As people ponder this question in their hearts, often long-buried dreams come to the surface, prompting a glimmer of hope or sadness. Then I ask, "What keeps you from attempting that dream?"

They usually identify some surface answers—too young, too old, don't have the money, don't have the time, or work too many hours. But underlying most of those reasons is often one basic emotion— *fear*. Fear of failure, rejection, hard work, sacrifice, or loneliness. The fears are many.

The truth is God plants dreams in all our hearts. If God has put a dream in your heart, there's going to be some fear in living it out. The more God-sized the dream, the greater the fear because anything great done for God means stepping out of our comfort zone. Our children will have those same big dreams in their hearts. As parents we have the opportunity to advance the kingdom of God by raising children who will boldly, in spite of the fear at times, obey the call and follow the dreams God has given them.

Memory Verses

Have I not commanded you? Be strong and courageous.
Do not be terrified; do not be discouraged, for the
LORD your God will be with you wherever you go.

JOSHUA 1:9

I sought the LORD, and He answered me;
he delivered me from all my fears.

PSALM 34:4

For God hath not given us the spirit of fear; but
of power, and of love, and of a sound mind.

2 TIMOTHY 1:7 KJV

Cast all your anxiety on him because he cares for you.

1 PETER 5:7

"Because he loves me," says the LORD, "I will protect
him; I will protect him, for he acknowledges my name."

PSALM 91:14

Now I know that the LORD saves his anointed; he
answers him from his holy heaven with the saving power
of his right hand. Some trust in chariots and some in
horses, but we trust in the name of the LORD our God.

PSALM 20:6-7

Encouraging Words

*The greatest mistake we make is living in
constant fear that we will make one.*

—JOHN MAXWELL

In God we trust.

—MOTTO ON UNITED STATES CURRENCY

*Don't be afraid to go out on a limb.
That's where the fruit is.*

—H. JACKSON BROWNE

*When a man has quietly made up his mind that there
is nothing he cannot endure, his fears leave him.*

—GROVE PATTERSON

*Avoiding danger is no safer in the long run than outright
exposure. Life is either a daring adventure, or nothing.*

—HELEN KELLER

Discussion or Journal Questions

1. Where do you stand on the scale of fear impacting your life—one being not at all, ten being fear-driven?

2. Write down a list of your fears about the future. Identify those that seem like "giants."

3. Do you see your fears affecting your child in any way? Describe.

4. How do fears affect our faith?

5. List some of the attributes of God that remind you of how powerful God is in the face of your fears (unchanging, all-knowing, and so forth).

6. Read Psalm 20:6-7. This passage talks about trusting in horses and chariots instead of God. What are some examples of "horses" and "chariots" in your life?

7. Why do we choose to trust in things other than God?

8. When have you seen God's protection in a fearful situation? What have you seen His hand provide for your basic needs?

9. Why do you think God sometimes waits for us to make the first move?

10. What would you do for God if you knew you wouldn't fail?

Chapter Five

Managing Stress

London Bridge is falling down…

To the untrained eye, Ruth is a normal second grader. She likes Hannah Montana, plays with dolls, and dreams of what her bedroom would look like if she were a princess. Look closer and you'll see something else about Ruth that is an ongoing cause of stress. She's a perfectionist.

As her mother, I denied this vehemently when a teacher pointed it out. "A perfectionist!" I gasped. "You should see her bedroom!" The teacher kindly overlooked my un-mother-like response and went on to describe the behavior she saw Ruth exhibit in the classroom. It seemed that Ruth frequently worried over her papers and was willing to miss recess in order to finish them right. In fact she was so afraid of making a mistake that she would erase and re-erase until it was perfect—at least in her mind.

I pondered this assessment and considered if I had missed something. It hadn't crossed my mind that Ruth might be a perfectionist. The product of Ruth's efforts didn't reflect my preconceived notions of perfect. However, the reality is Ruth has trouble finishing a project because of her own unrealistic expectations of herself. Her behavior was definitely changing as the school year progressed, and we struggled to uncover the cause.

Ruth did seem to work longer on her papers than necessary. She took longer than anyone in the family to finish a simple task. She also has trouble making a decision—whether it's buying a gift for a friend or what to eat at a restaurant. Until hearing the teacher's comment, I thought it was just dawdling and distraction. Now I see it as a child who is so concerned with doing things just right that she's stuck in neutral. Add to the mix that she struggles with attention, short-term memory issues, and has two parents who experience ongoing frustration with her delays and forgetfulness, and we've got one stressed-out kid.

What Is Stress?

We all know the word stress. Though we may have trouble pinpointing a definition, we know it when we feel it. We connect it with an overloaded schedule, worry over things we can't control, and collapsing on the living room couch with a bag of chips in one hand and the remote control in the other. Stress causes me to head for coffee, while other people handle it in more spiritually mature ways.

So what is stress? In the scientific world of mechanics, stress is the internal resistance, or counterforce, of a material to the effects of an external force. That's a technical definition with a simple application to stress in our lives. Stress happens when we respond physically or emotionally to outside pressure. And pressure is something we all experience to some degree, though not always negatively.

From a very early age, we feel pressure to get along with others, to obey our parents, and to eat our veggies. As school starts, the external pressure ramps up, complete with deadlines for assignments, tests, and strict behavior expectations. Then change gets added to the mix: a new house, sibling, school, or parent. Change forces us to adapt to a new definition of normal.

No matter how carefree we think childhood is in comparison to adulthood, children still face many stressors in the early years. Hopefully as adults we apply coping skills we have learned over time. We even have the authority to make decisions on what stress we allow into our lives. Children, on the other hand, have neither the coping skills nor authority. Consequently, when faced with an ever increasing amount of pressure in their lives, children are often victims of circumstance.

Here's an everyday example of how even a joyful event can create a stressful situation for a child. Imagine the day Mom and Dad bring child number two home from the hospital. Child number one faces a surprising amount of external change and pressure:

- He needs to share his parents' attention and love.
- There's more noise in the house.
- He may give up his crib and move to a "big-boy bed."
- There is new furniture in the house—like a swing and baby rocker.
- He may even give up his place in the car.
- He may need to help with the baby or around the house.
- Even the smells are different.

His little mind and body are forced to react to this change. He didn't have a choice about whether he got a sister or brother, and he may or may not have wanted one. Nevertheless, little brother will experience stress because of this new household member. Some children respond better than others, but to deal effectively with stress, we should learn to adapt and move on to become a more well-rounded, capable, and, hopefully, loving person.

So what's the problem? Stress is just a fact of life that everyone needs to deal with. Right? That's true. The problem comes when one of three things happen in anyone's life:

1. The pressures *accumulate faster* than our ability to adapt or respond.
2. The pressures *last longer* than our ability to maintain control.
3. Our internal makeup is simply *unable to deal with* the stress.

When I look at those three categories, it is startlingly obvious to me that children are at even greater risk for experiencing negative stress than adults. This is especially true because children have very little control over their environments and the pressures therein.

It is incumbent upon parents to guide their children in making healthy decisions and enforcing disciplines to enable them to face their stress and overcome it rather than succumb to it. In my daughter's case, too much pressure overwhelms her. As her parent, it's my job to remove as much pressure as possible. For Ruth that means fewer activities until her emotional development and experience catch up to her interests.

The Causes of Stress in Children

Clinical Psychiatry News published a survey that was taken in 2005 regarding the top stress triggers that nine- to thirteen-year-old children face. Here are the results:

Grades/school/homework	36%
Family	32%
Friends/teasing/gossip	21%
Siblings	20%
Mean/annoying people	20%
Parents	14%
Yelling/loud noises	9%
Fighting	9%
Sports	8%
Lack of autonomy	7%[1]

While some of these stresses are avoidable, most of them are part of life. It's interesting that all but two of the stressors involve people. It's sad that the gift of community God gave us at creation is such a source of stress. Because God calls us to love people, helping our children deal with interpersonal relations should be a top priority, but that's a topic for another book.

The Signs of Stress

When our son Robbie was three, we visited a playground near our home. There were children climbing all over the jungle gym like ants over a gumdrop, and my three boys were somewhere in the mix. Happy shrieks and giggles filled the air, as children raced up the stairs, down the slides, and in circles around each other.

Suddenly, amid the cheerful sounds of play, the piercing sound of pain reached my ears. I instinctively knew that the cry came from Robbie, and I quickly scanned the play equipment until I found him, crumpled in a heap on the sand, holding his foot. Apparently he was waiting for his turn at the fireman's pole when he was accidentally shoved from behind and hit the ground too hard.

My husband scooped him up and carried him to a bench as Robbie continued to sob. Robbie was a tough little guy, so when the crying continued for 30 minutes we knew something was wrong. We drove him to an urgent care center where we filled out the paperwork and waited in the waiting room for the doctor. After about 15 minutes of waiting, Robbie fell asleep in my arms.

He slept through the X-ray, he slept while we waited for results, and he slept through our meeting with the doctor where we learned Robbie had broken a bone in his foot. I asked the doctor how my son, who was in such pain just an hour earlier, could be sound asleep. The doctor answered matter-of-factly, "He ran out of adrenaline. When he got hurt, his body released a rush of adrenaline, and now it needs to replenish itself."

That explanation made sense to me. It also explains many of the physical symptoms children experience with stress. When adults are under stress, adrenaline actually helps us perform better. Children have a different response. Georgia Witkin, author of *KidStress,* makes this observation, "When the fight-or-flight response pumps the hormone adrenaline into their little bodies, they've got even more energy. But unlike adults, who may have learned how to channel that energy productively or at least have developed various coping strategies, children 'act up' as we say."[2] Kids under stress may experience behavioral problems, moodiness, irritability, whining, crying, restlessness, or inability to sleep.

When the adrenaline runs out, children might be excessively tired, withdraw from normal activities, and have physical symptoms like a cold or flu.[3] Kids also routinely experience headaches and stomachaches from stress. To help identify a pattern, keep a journal of symptoms. If your child has a stomachache every Thursday night (before a Friday quiz), you are probably dealing with some sort of nervous reaction.

However, it's imperative to mention if your child consistently experiences any physical symptoms. Please visit a doctor to rule out a serious underlying medical issue.

Learn to Deal with Stress

Because stress is unavoidable, it is in our children's best interest to help prepare them to deal with the pressure. As Mary Southerland, author of *Escaping the Stress Trap*, says, "We must be *ready* to deal with stress before we are *required* to deal with stress. Dealing with stress is an ongoing, daily battle that will not end this side of heaven."[4]

Southerland doesn't think we can point to one solution to the problem of stress. Instead it requires a broad approach to all areas of our lives. Take an honest look at all aspects of your child's life and consider where you can make changes.

Practical Tips for Creating a Stress-Free Day at Home

A few years ago, I couldn't get our mornings under control. I was a mess, and so were the kids. I thought I was doing them a favor by letting them sleep a few minutes longer, allowing them to watch cartoons while they ate a quick breakfast, and then hurrying them off to school. To say our mornings were chaotic was an understatement, and half the time someone left the house angry. On those days peace was a false product as I fought to hold my frustration under tight control.

The day I mindlessly pointed the remote control at two kids arguing at the breakfast table and clicked to turn them off was the breaking point. From that point on, we established a schedule with specific times for waking up, eating breakfast, getting ready, and leaving the house. We turned the television permanently off in the morning! What a difference.

After school we developed a firm schedule that included homework and playtime. From Sunday night to Friday afternoon, there is no "screen time." Unless a homework assignment requires the computer, we turn off everything with a screen during those days. Not only does our schedule run smoother, but arguments have dramatically decreased.

My husband and I realized what we considered a privilege (watching television or playing a video game) our children considered a right. This mindset created an underlying cause of stress when our schedule was haphazard. For us managing media time is critical for limiting stress at home.

Other tips for managing stress include eliminating hurry. For years I was always in a rush. I'd try to squeeze in one more little task before leaving and consistently underestimated what it would take to get my children ready and in the car. I'd race in to a meeting or event at the last minute (after rushing my kids out of the car) and paste on a fake smile as if I was the most relaxed mother in the world. Little did anyone know the stress we'd all been under due to my last-minute tasks. My children sure paid the price for my hurry.

Now I set a quitting time far ahead of when I need to leave. I ask my children and myself, "What do we absolutely need to get done before we leave?" Everything else is set aside, and we focus on the task at hand. We've come to recognize how important it is to have a stress-free family experience, and I am finally modeling how to build in margins to our schedule so we experience more peace throughout the week.

Two final practical tips include getting enough sleep and holding to a proper diet. Every child's sleep needs are different, but basically all children should get between eight and ten hours a night. Set an early bedtime, and you'll have a much more pleasant day. Plus, children need a well-balanced diet. This might mean creating a menu for the week and filling in places for your children to get all their requirements for dairy, protein, fruits, and vegetables.

Most of us live on a diet with too many carbohydrates (such as cereals, potatoes, and breads). While we need these items, we should eat them along with the other food groups. A breakfast of toast, cereal, and a Pop-Tart will have your child's blood sugar and energy crashing before lunch. Adding protein to their morning breakfast will extend their energy until they eat again. See your child's pediatrician for suggestions on portion sizes and the number of daily servings recommended in the different food groups.

Home should be a stress-free haven for our children. It should be a place where they walk in and sigh, "I'm home." We can give our children a launching and landing pad of peace and security by establishing stress-free routines in a peaceful setting.

Overcommitment

Opportunities abound for our children, and most devoted parents want to give their children everything they missed. However, there is a grave danger in signing up for every "good" opportunity—our children become overcommitted.

Childhood is the time to try all sorts of new hobbies, sports, and activities. It's during this time that children explore their God-given design. Strengths become evident. Talent is revealed. There is joy in discovering a love for music or sports. Leadership skills emerge. Our children should explore these interests in moderation and preferably one at a time.

I remember when my children first started eating solid food. The doctor advised us to try one new food at a time and only give that food for a few days. That way we could isolate an allergy if there was one. We can apply this practice to our children and their activities. An overcommitted child might respond negatively to something new— not based on the activity itself, but because they feel overwhelmed. For example, a child who starts piano lessons, dance, and Girl Scouts all at the same time may resent the piano practice because it infringes on more fun activities. She may ask to quit piano, saying she doesn't like it. The truth may be she's just overcommitted. I wonder how many children have given up on something valuable because their little hearts and minds couldn't handle the stress at the time?

Overcommitment causes our lives to grow more shallow. We may have opportunities to try new things, but we never experience a measure of accomplishment. It's my goal for my children to have deeper and richer lives rather than busier lives. This starts by limiting their activities during the week.

Rick Warren writes, "It is impossible to do everything people want you to do. You have just enough time to do God's will."[5] A life of overcommitment invites our children to depend upon their achievements for their value instead of God. Starting a lifelong habit of prayer before making a commitment to a new activity will help your child make God-honoring and stress-free decisions.

Overwhelmed with Responsibilities

David Allen, author of *Getting Things Done*, sees a concerning trend in today's world. He writes:

> A paradox has emerged in this new millennium: people have enhanced quality of life, but at the same time they are adding to their stress levels by taking on more than they have resources to handle...And most people are to some degree frustrated and perplexed about how to improve the situation.[6]

There are times in a child's life when responsibilities weigh them down. They don't have to be doing a lot. What they have on their plate just might be too much. For whatever reason, they are stuck in this level of stress for a time. This happens to all of us. Even the most organized and wisest person finds herself overwhelmed with responsibilities from time to time. Our inability to process all that information at once causes stress about what we *aren't* doing.

Allen observes, "The big problem is that your mind keeps reminding you of things when you can't do anything about them. It has no sense of past or future. That means that as soon as you tell yourself that you need to do something and store it in your RAM, there's a part of you that thinks you should be doing that something *all the time*."[7]

As soon as we have two tasks stored in our minds, we generate a sense of personal failure because we can't do them both at once. This is the cause of much underlying stress for children and adults—they just can't put their finger on it. It causes an inability to fully relax, which then causes their stress level to rise.

An easy solution according to Allen is to get your responsibilities out of your head and down on paper. Once you have put your responsibilities in a trusted place, your mind relaxes. As our children's responsibilities increase, we can teach this concept of capturing information. It doesn't really matter where it gets stored—sticky notes, index cards, spiral notebooks, or a computer—but getting it out of our heads and putting it somewhere safe is a great solution.

Break Down a Task Together

For eight years my husband and I led the senior high group at our church. We loved those kids, and because we didn't have children at the time, we invested our lives in them. Our group was a close-knit community, and we shared many personal concerns with each other.

One Sunday night, as we sat in a circle at closing time, a young girl, who was a high achiever and model student, burst into tears. We could tell something was obviously wrong because this young lady was normally a model of confidence. We waited for her to gather her composure, while we worried about the cause of the breakdown. Maybe something was horribly wrong with her parents or brother. We loved her whole family and were immediately concerned.

Finally, with tears still dripping down her cheeks, she raised her head and said, "How will I know which pans to use when I'm married?"

I wanted to laugh aloud with relief, but that would have been highly inappropriate given the seriousness of her concern. This stressed-out girl from a loving family was overwhelmed with all the responsibilities facing her at the time. All of them were normal and good—there were just a lot. She was approaching graduation, and the reality of living on her own must have saturated her thoughts. Finally the idea of one more responsibility put her over the edge.

So we took a few minutes and addressed the topic of cooking. I explained that when it was time for her to cook, for herself or for another person, she wouldn't need to know everything. I told her stores sell cookware in sets, and if she followed a recipe, it would tell her what type of pan to use. Within minutes an overwhelming responsibility was broken down into a few manageable steps.

When our family moved from Phoenix to North Carolina, the North Carolina educational system was about a year ahead of where my children were academically. Josh started in second grade, and the teacher assigned a report in the first couple of weeks of school. He had no idea how to write a report. Back in Phoenix he was barely writing sentences at the end of first grade. After writing a note to the teacher and explaining the situation, Josh and I sat down and made a list of what he would need to do to finish the report. It still wasn't easy for him, but it didn't feel overwhelming with a list of doable steps.

Breaking down a task is easy for me because I think that way. However, many people have a big-picture view of a project. That's great for casting a vision, but less helpful for identifying the steps to get there. If that's you, invite a detail-oriented friend to help assess your child's situation and break it down into bite-sized pieces.

If a large project overwhelms your child, consider writing down each step of the project on a three-by-five-inch index card and number the cards in the order the steps should be completed. Small bites are easier to chew when dealing with a big responsibility.

Build in Time to Relax and Listen

Dylan is driven. He identifies a goal and plows full steam ahead. Whether it's academics or sports, Dylan is hardwired to achieve. So when he shows signs of stress, we take it seriously. We don't want him to become a type A personality or a heart-attack victim by the age of

30. For this high school sophomore, we've had to enforce down time. We don't allow any sports in the summer. We honor the Sabbath. We make sure he has time to play.

We also help plan times when he doesn't need to do anything except what he wants to do. Allowing him to make his own choices about when he eats and what he eats (with guidelines) is a great stress reliever for a child like this.

Just this week Dylan came home from school wanting to change a class. It was honors geometry and it was just too hard he said. He wanted to go to regular geometry. He slouched in his chair as he spoke and wouldn't meet my eyes. "Tell me about it," I said.

"I don't know," he replied and stared out the window. We sat in silence.

"Dylan," I offered, "if you want to change the class, you can change the class." More silence.

Finally he answered, "I don't want to drop the class, I just wanted to…"

"Vent?" I suggested.

"Yeah," he said with a grin.

Sometimes a listening ear helps more than a plan of attack.

Biblical Response to Stress

If you believe you've had a stressful day, wait 'til you hear about Elijah. His story is found in the book of First Kings.

At that time Ahab was king of Israel, but instead of being a godly king, he was wicked. In fact, he set up an altar to Baal in God's temple. The Bible says, "Ahab also made an Asherah pole and did more to provoke the LORD, the God of Israel, to anger than did all the kings of Israel before him" (1 Kings 16:33). Ahab married Jezebel, who worshipped Baal and hated the prophets of God. In fact, it was her goal to kill them all.

So when we read that Elijah starts his day by approaching King Ahab, we know there's trouble brewing. God told Elijah to present himself to Ahab, and Elijah obeyed.

Through Elijah, God gave a message for Ahab that day. He wanted Ahab to choose whom to follow. No longer would the Lord tolerate His people worshipping a false god. So Elijah called for 450 prophets of Baal to show up on Mount Carmel, and he faced them with the people of Israel watching. Then he asked for two bulls. The prophets of Baal cut one into pieces and put them on wood, and Elijah did the same to the other. Neither was to light the wood. Then Elijah said, "You call on the name of your god, and I will call on the name of the Lord. The god who answers by fire—he is God" (1 Kings 18:24).

The prophets of Baal called upon their god all day. They even shouted and danced around the altar—but no answer came. Then it was Elijah's turn. Elijah built a trench around the altar and poured 12 large jars of water over the altar. Everything was soaked. With a prayer Elijah called on God, and fire lit the sacrifice and burned everything. The Israelites fell down and worshipped God.

Elijah then called for the Israelites to round up the 450 prophets of Baal and take them to the Kishon Valley to slaughter them. Elijah's day wasn't over yet. God then showed Elijah that rain was coming and that King Ahab needed to get back to Jezreel before it arrived. While King Ahab hitched up his chariot, Elijah hitched his cloak into his belt and with supernatural power ran all the way back to Jezreel ahead of the chariot—over 20 miles!

Talk about an overwhelming day! But it still wasn't over. After King Ahab returned to his home, he told his wife Jezebel what happened. She was so angry she sent a letter to Elijah, threatening to kill him the next day. Instead of boldly facing this new threat, the Bible says, "Elijah was afraid and ran for his life" (1 Kings 19:3). Elijah journeyed a day into the desert to get away, sat down under a tree, asked God to kill him, and fell asleep.

What happened to God's hero? How could a man so confident and bold, collapse at the threat of one woman. Elijah was stressed—emotionally and physically. Although he had watched God perform unbelievable miracles through him just a few days earlier, he was overwhelmed and exhausted.

It's in the next few paragraphs that we find God's response to His servant's stress. In that response we find wisdom to help our children during times of their own stress.

Instead of allowing Elijah to escape his worries, the Lord sends an angel to wake him. The angel provides food and water and *then* allows Elijah to sleep. After a time of sleep and more nourishment, God calls Elijah to journey into the desert where he experiences a time of fellowship with God.

The story of Elijah shows us that when circumstances collide, even the most confident individual can become stressed out. Elijah was discouraged beyond his ability to cope. With God's loving care, God allowed Elijah time to recover with food and sleep. Then God called Elijah to a time away from his duties, allowing him to refocus on his priorities. God met Elijah in a tender way during that time, speaking to him in a calming gentle whisper. After that God called Elijah back into service.

We can apply this recovery process to our children when they experience overwhelming stress. Provide nourishment and protect their time of rest. To the best of your ability, remove outside pressure for a time to allow your child to recover with God's help. Encourage your child to read Scripture or listen to worship music. Create a calming atmosphere for your child to receive God's healing.

God doesn't want our children giving up or collapsing into depression or illness due to stress. He already has a plan for their restoration and that includes focusing on God's best for their lives, and resting in His presence.

Memory Verses

Therefore do not worry about tomorrow,
for tomorrow will worry about itself. Each
day has enough trouble of its own.

MATTHEW 6:34

God is our refuge and strength, an
ever-present help in trouble.

PSALM 46:1

The Lord is my shepherd, I shall not want.

PSALM 23:1 NKJV

Teach us to realize the brevity of life, so
that we may grow in wisdom.

PSALM 90:12 NLT

I will provide their needs before they ask, and I will
help them while they are still asking for help.

ISAIAH 65:24 NCV

Encouraging Words

When you are at the end of your rope,
tie a knot and hang on.

—ELEANOR ROOSEVELT

I believe God is managing affairs and that He
doesn't need any advice from me. With God in
charge, I believe everything will work out for the
best in the end. So what is there to worry about.

—HENRY FORD

Any concern too small to be turned into a prayer
is too small to be made into a burden.

—CORRIE TEN BOOM

Do not be afraid of tomorrow; for God is already there.

—AUTHOR UNKNOWN

Discussion or Journal Questions

1. What are the top causes of stress in your life?

2. Think about your normal day. Is there a time that is more stressful than others? What steps can you take to reduce the stress during this time?

3. Why are so many people overwhelmed with their responsibilities?

4. Because people can cause much stress, can you identify specific people your child might need to stay away from?

5. Does sibling conflict create stress in your house? Take some time to identify the biggest conflicts. Break them down into specific incidents or problems and create a plan to address them.

6. How does God give us direction for our lives so we aren't overwhelmed and stressed?

7. Identify some spiritual disciplines that you and your family could incorporate that would help to reduce stress in all your lives. (I recommend John Ortberg's *The Life You've Always Wanted* for an enjoyable approach to spiritual disciplines.)

8. Read 1 Kings 19:11-12. How did God reveal His presence to Elijah? Do you think God chose this approach for a reason, given Elijah's condition?

9. Is there anything you might change about how you speak or act that would reduce the stress in your life and your child's life?

10. Are their other practices your family needs to change to reduce the stress? Identify them and pray about how to make those changes.

Chapter Six

The Pain of Loneliness

Little Jack Horner sat in the corner...

Joshua sat facing the back of the couch. His head rested on his crossed arms, as he stared out the window. His little head moved from left to right as he watched two neighbor boys race past on bikes, shouting words of encouragement to each other and laughing at a shared joke.

I watched my second-grade son from the kitchen door, drying my hands with a dish towel. My shoulders dropped as Josh took a deep breath and let it out in a despairing sigh. Mirroring his sadness, my throat tightened and hot tears burned my eyes. Throwing the dish towel into the sink, I quietly stepped to the couch and slipped down next to him. Without saying a word, I enveloped his little frame with my arms and scooped him onto my lap.

His face nuzzled mine, and our tears mixed together. I could almost feel the wishing and hoping pulse through his small body: *Will they stop by* my *house? Will they invite* me *to play?* A smothered sob escaped from my little boy who was trying valiantly to be big.

Ever since our move to North Carolina earlier in the year, Joshua had trouble making friends. The playgroups were established, leaving my shy son painfully on the outside. His little brothers were good companions at home, but that didn't replace friendships at school or in the neighborhood.

The loneliness was oppressive, and I felt it too. I struggled greatly through that emotionally dark time. We all left lifelong friends when our family moved away from Phoenix. Our friendships at home had been born of common experiences and years spent together. They were effortless. Now we faced unknown territory, not just geographically but culturally and socially. This was a new world to us, and Josh felt it as painfully as I did.

It was a helpless feeling. A part of me wanted to march out on the street and demand that those children play with my son. But there are some things you just can't force or do for your kids, and friendships are high on that list. When children are very young, they will play with anyone, but around seven years old, that changes. I couldn't just plan a playdate anymore. Joshua needed more help than a trip to the park.

Up until that point, I'd taken this area of my son's life for granted. But no more. Joshua needed tools that would help him throughout the coming years face new situations and new relationships. Because I couldn't *make* the other children reach out to Josh, we had to have a different approach. This started with a single statement that became our family's guiding principle: To have a good friend, you need to be a good friend.

I'm happy to report that, as of the writing of this book, my son is a senior in high school with good friends. He has learned the qualities of being a good friend and has received the blessing of faithful friends in return. But it took years of practicing our good-friend principle.

Overcoming loneliness means making connections. God created us to live in relationship with one another, and for some children, this takes extra effort. Regardless of your child's natural bent, learning how to develop relationships is a skill that pleases God. When His children relate to and serve one another in love, not only does that please God, but good friendships are made. Friendship also has a long-term, positive impact on our health and well-being. Helping your child overcome loneliness by teaching him friendship skills is an excellent investment of time and effort on your part. I'm confident the tools that helped Josh can help most children.

Why Friendships Are Important

At creation God created man to need human interaction. The book of Genesis records God's words after creating Adam: "It is not good for the man to be alone" (Genesis 2:18). Creating Eve wasn't an after-thought. God didn't make a mistake by only creating Adam and then have to make it right by adding Eve. From the beginning God intended to create two. Although this is a picture of the marriage relationship, it still shows we are hardwired with a need for each other.

I believe God designed us to live in community with each other for a variety of reasons. One is God knew we would need each other to face the trials that life brings.

Although this is difficult to understand from a human perspective, God knew the future when He created Adam and Eve. Scripture tells us God is all-knowing, so He must have known that Adam and Eve would allow sin to enter the world. Thus, God knew we would need each other to stand strong.

Ecclesiastes 4:9-10 tells us, "Two are better than one, because they have a good return for their work: If one falls down, his friend can help him up. But pity the man who falls and has no one to help him up!" With Satan as our enemy and sin as our nature, we are weakened. Friends offer us help and protection.

Nature reveals this truth every year. In a forest, frost is more likely to damage a tree if it is standing alone. However, when the trees grow close together there is a natural protection, and they survive the cold.

Human contact can also be a lifeline during times of dark loneliness. One extreme example happened during the Vietnam War. American prisoners of war developed an ingenious way of communicating, even when locked in different cells. They tapped out a code, one that North Vietnamese jailers were never able to break. In the Hanoi Hilton, the code worked so well that prisoners even told each other jokes. And every Sunday, at a signal, the prisoners all stood—or attempted to stand—and together recited the Lord's Prayer and the Pledge of Alle-giance. Having friends who will encourage us when life is tough can mean the difference between giving up and persevering.

The prayer of our friends is also powerful. James 5:16 tells us, "There-fore confess your sins to each other and pray for each other so that you may be healed. The prayer of a righteous man is powerful and effective." This verse indicates the connection between the prayers of others and our healing.

Friends are good for our health. The Harvard Heart Letter of January 2007 reported, "Loneliness actually stresses the heart and the entire cardiovascular system, and may harm them as much as high blood pressure or high cholesterol...People with rich social networks generally live longer, recover faster from heart attacks and other health setbacks, and have more joyful lives."[1]

Helping our children become and find good friends is a valuable investment of our time. Not only do friends ease our loneliness, but they are a God-given answer to many of our lifetime spiritual, physical, and emotional needs.

Be a Good Friend First

If your child is in second grade or above, ask her who the popular kids are in her neighborhood, class, or school, and she'll probably provide a list. She'll also know whether or not she is part of that elite group.

If you're like me, the idea of a "popular" kid bothers you. It always means someone is left out. In my idyllic world, no one would sit on the sidelines wishing someone would invite them to play. Thankfully there's already a place like that. It's called heaven.

Even though most of us cringe at the idea of popularity, author Hara Estroff Marano believes there is a widespread misunderstanding about the topic and peer relationships in children. Popularity isn't a state randomly assigned at birth. Instead Marano claims popularity is a collection of qualities, attributes, and behavioral skills that are the foundation for successful human interaction throughout life.

Marano concludes, "The ability to form close friendships and maintain contact with others is a natural countercheck against most of the ways the mind can go off track. It is the closest thing to insurance against loneliness, one of the most physically and emotionally destructive of human conditions and one of the greatest sources of stress."[2]

Popularity for the sake of popularity would be harmful to a child. However, we can all learn something from children or adults who have good social skills and the ability to make strong interpersonal connections at any age.

Studies with teachers both in the classroom and on the playground show there are some specific attributes that attract children to other children. Marano identified the following positive characteristics of popular kids:

- Helpful
- Kind
- Sharing
- Cooperative
- Responsive to distress, empathetic

Interestingly these characteristics reflect common biblical mandates for all of us. Jesus spoke these words, "A new command I give you: Love one another. As I have loved you, so you must love one another." Paul gives the following instructions in Romans 12:10, "Be devoted to one another in brotherly love. Honor one another above yourselves." And in Philippians 2:3, Paul encourages us to, "Do nothing out of selfish ambition or vain conceit, but in humility consider others better than yourselves."

As Christians God calls us to an others-centered lifestyle. This must start very early, and it starts with parents. We can model this by reaching beyond our own four walls and serving extended family, friends, and strangers. We can practice compassion through simple acts of kindness like writing a letter, making a dinner, and picking flowers from our garden and taking them to a shut-in. Putting others' needs above our own should be an everyday practice for a follower of Jesus. As our children get involved, caring for others becomes natural.

Even the most timid child can learn to look beyond herself. As Christians we have the benefit of the Holy Spirit to empower and guide us. Parents also can have an enormous impact on their children.

Marano claims, "The more you believe that social competence depends on learnable skills, the more socially skilled your children will be."[3]

When someone reaches out to me, I'm immediately drawn to her. So it just makes sense that when our children reach out to others with loving motives, others will be drawn to them. Not only are they building a social network, they are practicing the love of God. It's a win-win situation.

The Skill of Conversation

Every parent knows the frustration of asking a child, "How was your day?" only to be answered, "Good." We may have heard that comes with the territory. I think it may have more to do with how the parent posed the question.

Good conversation, even for adults, isn't always easy. Learning to ask carefully thought-out questions may take advance planning. We can even make it a game for the little ones.

Good conversation usually starts with small talk. As adults we might talk about the weather, a television show, or an outfit someone is wearing. In this stage we practice polite rules of conversation, such as looking the other person in the eye, paying attention, and allowing her to respond without interrupting. When speaking with someone who is polite and interested, we naturally want to continue.

We carry on small talk normally with our children, but we are often doing something else, like fixing dinner, folding clothes, or driving. To teach children these basic manners, try sitting down at a table with milk and cookies. Practice eye contact and affirming mannerisms, like nodding of the head and agreeing with the comment.

If there is a comfort level to continue, many conversations will lead into experiences, thoughts, and opinions. Obviously children will speak on very different topics, but the practical tips for carrying on a more significant conversation with another child can be very helpful to establish a friendship. Here are some helpful tools for talking with a friend:

1. Listen with your whole body. Show your friend that you are paying attention by facing her, leaning forward in your seat, and looking her in the eye.

2. Make a positive comment and follow it with a question. Examples: "I love your outfit. Where did you get it?" "Dave, you're great at soccer. How long have you been playing?"

3. Show genuine interest in your friend. Ask about his life, family, likes, hobbies, and activities. The point of most conversations is to learn about the other person.

4. Ask open-ended questions when possible. Not, "Did you like the movie?" but, "What was your favorite part of the movie?"

5. Don't disagree in the beginning of a friendship. If your friend loved the part of the movie you disliked, don't volunteer that information. Keep the conversation positive.

It can be helpful to write out questions your child can use with friends. Have her memorize them rather than pull out the three-by-five card from her pocket on the playground. You might write questions like this:

- What did you do this weekend?
- What's your favorite sport to play? Why?
- What do you like best about school?
- What's your favorite thing to do on a Saturday morning?
- What's your favorite TV show?
- Tell me about your family.
- If you could decorate your room any way you want, what would you do?
- What would your favorite dinner include?

- If you won the lottery, what would you do with the money?
- If you could give away $1000, who would you give it to?

Be an Inviter

One of my best friends when my kids were young was Becky Smyth. Becky and her husband, Dean, attended our church, and we had our first children within a few months of each other. As our children grew, Becky was always coming up with an interesting activity and inviting others to join her. Two events that stand out most in my mind included a city-bus ride downtown with a stop at a children's museum and a trip to a horse ranch, where there were foals. Both were inexpensive and creative.

Becky and Dean were also great hosts with a heart for hospitality. They would plan a dinner, then invite different people to join them. The iced tea was always cold and the chili, hot, while friendships formed around their table. I learned a simple principle of friendship from Becky—be an inviter. This principle easily extends to children as they build friendships.

Help your child think of activities she could do with a friend, and then extend an invitation. This could include things at home like:

- Make and decorate cupcakes
- Paint flowerpots
- Make jewelry
- Build a model car
- Assemble a puzzle
- Play football, soccer, or Frisbee
- Make homemade greeting cards
- Make a scrapbook from summer vacation photos

You might also plan outings so your child can invite a friend. Some inexpensive outings or activities might include a:

- Skate park
- Swimming pool
- Picnic at a park
- Zoo
- Tour of a company (We've got a chocolate factory in our city, with free tours and samples.)
- Sporting event (High school, college, or farm leagues have inexpensive tickets.)
- Bike ride
- Children's event at a library
- Outdoor festival
- Free project for kids at a local hardware store (Our local Home Depot offers free classes.)
- Hike along a local trail
- Cultural center

Do your research and make a list of low-cost, family-friendly activities in your city. My husband and I purchased numerous travel guides for our state and other books that list activities for children. They are a great investment. Once you've got a list of interesting activities, schedule them on your family calendar, have your child invite a friend, and consider them an appointment that must be met.

Build Friendships Around Common Interests

One of the best ways to meet a friend is by doing something you enjoy. My kids met their best friends by getting involved in an activity they loved, such as playing music, football, soccer, or volunteering at church. The common interest is an immediate bond.

Finding and developing interests involve a learning process. It's best to ease into new experiences rather than investing $500 in equipment for a sport your child might not like in a month.

Your city's parks and recreation department might offer the most affordable ways to investigate a child's interest. For a nominal fee, you can sign up for a variety of classes. Here are some examples of classes offered in my area: ceramics, cheerleading, comic book drawing, golfing, hip-hop dancing, and Spanish.

Here are some other ways to invest in your child's interests:

- Encourage your child to take advantage of school programs and clubs.
- Check into larger churches in your area to see if they offer youth activities.
- Our national parks have junior ranger programs. See what's in your area at www.nps.gov.
- Check out your state parks.
- Get involved with the Boy Scouts and Girl Scouts.
- Sign up for a cooking class at a culinary school.
- Look into local museum programs.

The Highly Sensitive Child

Approximately one in five children is born with a highly sensitive nature. These children come across as shy or fearful and may be slow to warm up to people in a new situation. This nature is God-given and is a blessing in many ways. However, it can work against a child who longs to have friends but struggles to make them.

Because these children are sensitive to social nuances, they react to things other children would ignore. Overstimulation from noise or activity can produce a variety of responses, from withdrawing to crying.

Unfortunately for the sensitive child, these types of reactions tend to create tension with other children. It's hard for others to feel as if they have to walk on eggshells around your child for fear of what might upset them. Children thrive in predictable situations and relationships, and overly sensitive children can't always predict their own reactions.

For parents of a sensitive child, it's best to desensitize your child to a new situation when possible. Consider planning get-togethers with other children before school starts. Speak with your child's teachers, counselors, or leaders to provide opportunities for your child to work quietly when needed. If your child can communicate his most stressful times, find ways to walk through those situations together. This can build up your child's confidence with other people.

Talk to your child about her reactions in public settings. A sensitive child probably understands feelings and emotions better than most children. Explain how other children feel when she reacts (or overreacts). Her natural sense of empathy might help her respond differently in a stressful situation. She might also understand the importance of thinking the best of others and not taking their actions personally.

Friends Share Each Other's Burdens

There's a great scene in the movie *Lord of the Rings: The Return of the King*. Sam and Frodo approach the end of their long journey to destroy a ring that Frodo carries and restore peace to their embattled land. The two little hobbits pick their way up a volcano-like mountain with smoke and burning rock. Frodo is the carrier of the ring, and with each step, the evil forces behind it drain his will and strength. When it looks as if Frodo can carry his burden no farther, his faithful companion, Sam, lifts him in his arms and says, "Come on, Mr. Frodo. I can't carry it for you, but I can carry you." With that, solid little Sam picks up Frodo and carries him the rest of the way up the mountain.

As I watched that amazing scene, God showed me a picture of His vision for friendship, especially Christian friendship—friends helping each other when faced with life's difficulties. Although life is hard enough dealing with our own problems, a good friend steps forward, not backward, when someone is in trouble. This might be counterintuitive to a protective parent. When there is any trouble, my initial instinct is to tuck my children under my wings and hide them. However, as our children get older, they will have friends who have problems. Life is messy. Ministry to our friends is messy too. How your child reacts to a friend with a problem will be a defining moment.

There's a story in Luke 5 about four men who had a friend with a problem—he was paralyzed. Although they couldn't solve the problem, these friends knew who could. So with great faith and determination, they carried their friend to a house where Jesus was teaching. When they couldn't get through the door because of the crowds, they carried their friend up to the roof and lowered his mat through the tiles and into the center of the crowd, where Jesus did heal him.

One of the best ways to teach young children to care for others is to start with prayer. Instead of just discussing the problems of a friend, pray about them together. As your child gets older, he might offer to pray for the friend, invite him to church if he doesn't already attend one, purchase a Bible for the friend, or write down some Scriptures that apply to their situation.

When children enter their teens, carrying each other's burdens becomes even more challenging. As my oldest children have reached out to kids with troubled lives, I prayerfully trust them to God's protection—again. I fight that urge to draw them back into the safety of my protection. But I know this is part of growing up and childhood friendships transitioning into adult friendships.

Be Your Child's Friend

A woman wrote to Dr. James Dobson with a heart-wrenching question: "My child is often ridiculed and hurt by the other children on our block, and I don't know how to handle the situation. He gets very depressed and comes home crying frequently. How should I respond when this happens?"

Dr. Dobson's answer was simple and to the point: "When your child has been rejected in this manner, he is badly in need of a friend—and you are elected."[4]

Much has been written in the past few decades of the dangers of parents neglecting their disciplinary roles in favor of the "best friend" approach. Most parents understand that children need us to be parents first and friends second. But the role of friend can be a powerful one when helping your child deal with loneliness.

When your child is lonely, look for activities you can do together that are fun and healthy for both of you. Especially choose activities where you can talk. These are great times to practice the art of conversation.

The Benefit of Loneliness

Although loneliness is painful, it isn't always a bad place to be for a time. C.S. Lewis said, "God whispers to us in our pleasures, speaks to us in our conscience, but shouts in our pain. It is His megaphone to rouse a deaf world."

Perhaps there are times when God allows loneliness into our lives as an invitation to pursue Him as our closest friend. When our friends have left us or we have left them, God reveals His presence in new ways. He reminds us that He is always here. Tim Hansel, author of *Through the Wilderness of Loneliness*, writes, "Loneliness is not a time of abandonment…it just feels that way. It's actually a time of encounter at new levels with the only One who can fill that empty place in our hearts."[5]

God longs to fill the heart of your child with Himself. As adults we know how quickly we can fill the desires of our hearts with the things of this world. Many of us have learned that our attempts to find replacements for God are fleeting and insubstantial.

As your child faces a time of loneliness, take this opportunity to introduce Jesus as a best friend. Jesus Himself called us friends in John 15:15: "I no longer call you servants, because a servant does not know his master's business. Instead, I have called you friends, for everything that I learned from my Father I have made known to you."

When to End a Friendship

In 1999, the events at Columbine High School in Colorado stunned the world. On a seemingly normal day, two disturbed young men took the lives of 13 others and themselves.

As we learned about those who died through television, radio, and print media, the life of Cassie Bernall particularly struck a chord in my heart. Cassie was a beautiful girl who had become a Christian just two years earlier. Her words and actions on that horrible day brought honor to God. I sobbed thinking about her bravery and the loss her parents faced.

We also learned that Cassie walked a hard and dangerous road before becoming a Christian. When Cassie's parents discovered this, they took immediate action. This included pulling Cassie out of the public school and putting her in a Christian school, imposing constraints on all her activities, and even moving to another house. They did all this to keep her away from friends who had been a very bad influence. Two years later Cassie gave her life to Christ at a youth retreat, and her eternity was changed.

When I'm faced with making a decision in my children's best interest and I know it will make them angry, I remember those brave parents. I pray we never have to take such drastic action, but the time may come when parents need to make serious changes for their children's sake. As a loving and spirit-led parent, seek God's wisdom and the counsel of a trusted friend or pastor when you have a concern about your child's friends.

~

A child can experience loneliness in the midst of a group of friends, and a solitary child can be content. Loneliness grows in the heart and is not a social condition. The good news is God has already picked out a friend for your child. By helping your child develop the practices of being a good friend, you'll equip him or her for a lifetime of healthy, God-honoring relationships and chase away loneliness.

Memory Verses

*Greater love has no one than this, that
he lay down his life for his friends.*

JOHN 15:13

*If one falls down, his friend can help him up. But pity
the man who falls and has no one to help him up!*

ECCLESIASTES 4:10

*A new command I give you: Love one another.
As I have loved you, so you must love one
another. By this all men will know that you
are my disciples, if you love one another.*

JOHN 13:34-35

*A troublemaker plants seeds of strife;
gossip separates the best of friends.*

PROVERBS 16:28 NLT

*Let your conversation be always full of grace, seasoned
with salt, so that you may know how to answer everyone.*

COLOSSIANS 4:6

Encouraging Words

*The pain of loneliness is one way in
which (God) gets our attention.*

—ELISABETH ELLIOT

You can make more friends in two months by becoming more interested in other people than you can in two years by trying to get people interested in you.

—DALE CARNEGIE

Loneliness is the most terrible poverty.

—MOTHER TERESA

Loneliness is the first thing which God's eye named, not good.

—JOHN MILTON

To ease another's heartache is to forget one's own.

—ABRAHAM LINCOLN

Discussion or Journal Questions

1. Think about the best friend you ever had. What qualities did *you* display in that friendship?

2. What are the qualities of a friend that matter most to you now?

3. Identify your child's greatest strength as a friend.

4. Identify your child's greatest weakness as a friend.

5. If you could hand pick a friend for your child, what attributes (character, beliefs, involvement in specific activities) would be most important to you?

6. Consider those attributes from question five. Where would your child most likely meet a friend with those characteristics? Make a list and consider how to get your child involved.

7. What activities can you do as a family to develop the characteristics of a good friend in your child?

8. What attitudes or behaviors can hurt a friendship most?

9. What characteristics does God display when He reveals Himself to us as a friend?

10. What does God ask of us as His friend? Consider whether you fulfill those requirements or fall short.

11. What can you do to be a better friend to God?

Chapter Seven

Turning Failure into Victory

...ashes, ashes, we all fall down.

Michael Jordan was cut from his high school basketball team for lack of skill. Lucille Ball was dismissed from drama school and told she was too shy. Thomas Edison was told by a teacher he was too stupid to learn. Walt Disney was fired from his job at a newspaper because he had no good ideas. A music teacher told Beethoven he had no hope as a composer. Louis Pasteur was a mediocre student in undergraduate studies and ranked fifteenth out of twenty-two students in chemistry. Jesus Christ was falsely accused, arrested, and killed.

The disciples of Jesus must have been shattered that Friday. For three years they followed this man from Nazareth. They watched Him heal the sick, restore sight to the blind, and even raise people from the dead. When Jesus said, "I have come as Light into the world, so that everyone who believes in Me will not remain in darkness" (John 12:46 NASB), they got it. Darkness enveloped the hearts of their countrymen. They needed the Light.

Twelve ordinary men abandoned everything to follow Jesus—jobs, family, and homes—not with regret, but with hope. Hope for the promise Jesus offered. Look where it got them that Friday. Jesus was dead—they'd witnessed the crucifixion. Only eleven now, they must have gathered that night after scattering throughout the city. Other followers joined them to mourn the death of the man they loved and the death of the hope He offered.

On Saturday they were still together. No one left. Though they could have. They could have packed up their things and put this failed adventure behind them—back to fishing, back to family, back to normal. But no one left. In spite of what appeared to be the complete failure of this new kingdom, everyone stayed. Faithful.

Saturday inched forward to noon, dusk, and then evening. The beauty of the night sky didn't ease their pain. Perhaps they reminisced some. In hindsight Jesus wasn't really what they were expecting. When the prophets of old foretold a king would come to rescue them, they figured it would be someone imposing, with power, maybe with chariots even to whip their enemies into submission. Some took longer than others to readjust their expectations. But when God opened their eyes to the beauty of His plan, they bought into it with their lives.

They couldn't sleep. What were they thinking I wonder. Finally, in complete exhaustion, their tired bodies overtook their worried minds. Sunday morning dawned. I imagine some woke up hoping it was all a bad dream. Then reality settled in like heavy summer storm clouds. Jesus was still dead.

Two women got ready first and went to the tomb. Expecting to find the body of their beloved Savior, God treated them instead to a display of His power. With a violent earthquake shaking the ground, an angel of the Lord came from heaven, rolled back the stone covering the tomb, and sat down on the rock. *Hello!*

The angel looked at the women and spoke words that transformed them from hopeless to hope-filled:

> Do not be afraid, for I know that you are looking for Jesus, who was crucified. He is not here; he has risen, just as he said. Come and see the place where he lay. Then go quickly and tell his disciples: He has risen from the dead and is going ahead of you into Galilee (Matthew 28:5-7).

Can you even imagine the celebration? It had only *looked* like failure. Instead it was glorious victory! Hope wasn't dead. Jesus was alive!

The disciples learned a lesson they would never forget: When God is involved, things aren't always what they seem to be.

There's Always Hope When God Is Involved

The disciples of Jesus discovered early on in their ministry that God's ways were often beyond their understanding. The disciples wanted Jesus to send 5000 men home to eat, and instead Jesus suggested the disciples feed them with a handful of bread and fish. They expected Jesus to catch up to them in the middle of the lake via a boat, instead He strolled on the water. Every time the disciples expected Jesus to handle something in human strength, He called upon heavenly strength to solve the problem.

Today we see problems and failures with the same eyes as the disciples—even when we know that God is able to do things beyond what we can imagine. When we look at a failure, we often only see an ending. God, however, sees an opportunity for a new beginning.

Sometimes I catch myself limiting God. I even unconsciously pass this on to my children by not praying for certain things. We'll get past a rough time, and it will hit me that we didn't pray.

Jesus modeled a life of prayer, and God answered miraculously. Jesus not only invited His followers to pray about everything, He also told them to pray continuously. One of my favorite stories Jesus told was about the persistent widow. It's short, so I've included the entire passage:

> Then Jesus told his disciples a parable to show them that they should always pray and not give up. He said: "In a certain town there was a judge who neither feared God nor cared about men. And there was a widow in that town who kept coming to him with the plea, 'Grant me justice against my adversary.'
>
> "For some time he refused. But finally he said to himself, 'Even though I don't fear God or care about men, yet because this widow keeps bothering me, I will see that she gets justice, so that she won't eventually wear me out with her coming!'"

> And the Lord said, "Listen to what the unjust judge says. And will not God bring about justice for his chosen ones, who cry out to him day and night? Will he keep putting them off? I tell you, he will see that they get justice, and quickly. However, when the Son of Man comes, will he find faith on the earth?'" (Luke 18:1-8).

Jesus invited His followers to pray and not give up. This should be our battle plan on behalf of our children and with our children. God still performs miracles on our behalf. Let's invite Him to do so.

While prayer is the bedrock of turning what looks like a failure into a victory, parents can also implement other practices. Redefining failure is a challenge for everyone. We need to retrain our minds to accept failure as an invitation to try again.

Encourage Curiosity

Many successful people overcome failure because of a natural curiosity that sparks their ability to persist. Thomas Edison failed thousands of times while he was practicing on the light bulb! When people suggested he quit, he replied, "I have gotten lots of results! If I find 10,000 ways something won't work, I haven't failed. I am not discouraged because every wrong attempt discarded is often a step forward."

Thomas Edison was naturally curious. Apparently his incessant questions frustrated his teacher enough that Edison's mother began to homeschool her son. Edison's parents fed their son's inborn curiosity through books.

Today a parent can spark a child's curiosity by exposing him to a variety of experiences. This takes intentionality and persistence on a parent's part. Consider all the wonders of this world and pick one to start. God's creation is amazing. From the distant stars to the rocks under our feet, God made it all good.

Make an effort to engage all your child's senses as you explore. You never know when your child will discover a love of flowers from the smell or a love of baking from the taste. A parent can also encourage curiosity with prompting questions. For example, if your child is learning to make cookies, you might ask, "What would it taste like if you included another ingredient? What ingredient would you add?"

If you are exploring nature together, you might say, "I wonder what the valley would look like if we climbed a little higher." Instead of just saying, "Let's hike up the mountain," you've put a question in your child's mind.

Television producers use provocative statements to hook viewers' interest and entice viewers to tune in the next week to find out what happens. Writers know how to end a chapter so the reader can't put the book down. Parents can implement some of the same techniques to pique their child's interest in a variety of subjects and foster God-given curiosity.

Remove the Labels

We stumble and call ourselves "clumsy." We weigh a few pounds more than we did in high school and call ourselves "fat." We forget an appointment and call ourselves an "idiot."

The names we and others give ourselves have powerful implications. Consider the beauty in the names of Jesus in Isaiah's prophecies: "For to us a child is born, to us a son is given, and the government will be on his shoulders. And he will be called Wonderful Counselor, Mighty God, Everlasting Father, Prince of Peace."

Your child will undoubtedly have a label or two for herself when she fails. However, the only label she should use for herself is the one God gave her through her faith in Christ—chosen.

Claiming God's names for us counteracts the negative labels we (and others) put on us. Here are a few names your child can claim:

- Loved by God (John 15:12)
- Son/daughter (John 1:12)
- Friend (John 15:15)
- Citizen of heaven (Philippians 3:20)
- Blessed (Ephesians 1:3)
- Forgiven (Ephesians 1:7)

I know I've mentioned this in other places in the book, but it's important enough to include more than once. Understanding our position in Christ is spiritual armor when we experience life's many failures. We need to remove the negative names and proudly wear the names God gave us.

Set Realistic Goals

God asks us to be good stewards of the abilities He gave us. A good steward accepts a gift with a grateful heart, then sets about using it to her abilities. God doesn't lay out a grid of success standards. The parable of the talents found in Matthew 25 shows God is just as pleased with the servant who produced four talents as the one who produced ten. He's more concerned with obedience than numbers. We are the ones who define failure and success by an external influence of some kind, like an older sibling's experience.

Consider the child who tried out last year for the school play and didn't get a part. She stands in front of the music room looking at the list of parts. A nervous feeling starts churning in her gut. Is trying out worth the embarrassment of not getting a part? How does she define success? Is it getting any part? Or is it getting a specific part? Or maybe a lead part, like her sister did when she attended?

For the child who is afraid to try for fear of failure, consider setting a reachable goal. In the example of the play tryouts, success might be trying out. That act of courage is worth rewarding. Did you ever try your hardest, only to have no one notice? That in itself is discouraging. However, when a parent acknowledges effort, the child tries again.

Sometimes attitude goals can define success. When a child joins a sports team only to sit on the bench, we can celebrate his good attitude. In that instance the goal might be to encourage the other teammates. That takes the focus off the game and onto character development. No matter what it is, having a goal moves a person in the right direction, and sometimes that matters more than anything.

Train for Pain

When Dr. David Livingstone was working in Africa, a group of friends sent a letter saying, "We would like to send other men to you. Have you found a good road into your area yet?" Apparently Dr. Livingstone sent this message in reply, "If you have men who will only come if they know there is a good road, I don't want them. I want men who will come if there is no road at all."

Does God desire us to follow Him even when it seems impossible? Is He watching to see what we will do when we face a dead end or failure? I think so. He's looking for a follower He can trust to push on past discouragement when the going gets rough.

I often wonder why following God isn't easier. There are days when I'm just tired of getting called out of my comfort zone to obey God. On those days I've been known to whine in my prayers and ask God if there isn't any way I can serve Him from the safety of my recliner. But that's not God's way. God is too big and has too many things to accomplish to limit His plans by my desire for security and control.

Maybe there is something within us that is revealed when we are pressured from without. Maybe the call to obey shines light on the truth about our faith. I do know that to grow, God stretches my faith, and that's often uncomfortable.

Last year I started an exercise program and wanted to quit a month into it. It's probably because I'm the least athletic person I know. I've also been told I run worse than a girl, and I'm pretty sure I flunked the president's physical fitness test in grade school.

However, because I know in my head that exercise is the only path to getting stronger, I ignored my body's protests and pressed on. Each week I discovered a new pain somewhere in my body—my shins, knees, and arms all groaned with the discomfort of being awoken from their sedentary state.

During one grueling exercise class, the instructor had us do a lower back exercise. At the first twinge of pain, I stopped. I knew that some pain could be dangerous and didn't want to continue something that could be damaging to my back. Watching me stop, the instructor stooped down to my level with a questioning look on his face. "It hurts," I explained. "I know," he answered. "This exercise is going to strengthen your back. Stop when you need to rest but try it again. And each time, hold it just a little bit longer."

My first instinct was to stop at the painful feeling. However, in order to get stronger, I had to experience the pain. Pain seems to be a common side effect any time we try to strengthen an area of our lives. I'm sorry to admit that my instinct to avoid pain or discomfort has often kept me from achieving goals in my life. Part of this is because it's difficult to differentiate the pain that we should avoid, like getting burned from touching a stove and the kind of pain that makes us stronger. Pain just seems like pain—something to run from.

In parenting my children to overcome failure, I've had to deal with this issue myself. It's only in understanding how to push past all the devastating emotions of failure, that I've been able to counsel them in their darkest times. The pain of failure isn't permanent, but the regret of quitting is.

James 1:2-4 confirms the importance of developing resolve and pressing on: "Consider it pure joy, my brothers, whenever you face trials of many kinds, because you know that the testing of your faith develops perseverance. Perseverance must finish its work so that you may be mature and complete, not lacking anything." If the disciples needed to develop perseverance, then it must take practice, even for the most disciplined of us.

As I have pushed through the pain of life, especially discouragement and failure, God has revealed His faithfulness to me on the other side of the pain, time and time again. Obeying when God hasn't revealed the steps along the way or the final destination is challenging. But when we choose to walk by faith and not by sight, God gets all the glory in the end because we *know* we couldn't have done it on our own!

What Did You Learn?

Evaluating a failure is always painful. Who wants to relive a bad experience? Yet, successful people know the only way to improve is to review past performance. Athletes watch their games. Speakers listen to their talks. Singers record themselves. Authors edit, edit, and re-edit. Scientists record every experiment.

Reviewing our performance and dissecting it is how we grow. It's how we identify our weak areas, how we evaluate our strengths, and how we create a plan to get from here to where we want to be. In an earlier chapter on overcoming disappointment, I mentioned this same review process. However, in that instance my son made the jazz band, just not the level he aimed for. He didn't consider it a failure. We evaluated the situation, just not his performance. However, when a child feels she has failed, it is increasingly important to evaluate the performance.

Just trying again isn't always the answer. American author Dale Carnegie wrote, "The successful man will profit from his mistakes and try again in a different way." We can't repeat the same steps and expect a different result. We must try a new approach. It might be a new way of studying, practicing, reacting, conversing, cooking, building, or assembling. It doesn't have to be completely different—just tweaked.

God Works Everything for Our Good

Moses was an obedient man of God who might have felt like a failure. After leading the grumbling Israelites in the desert for 40 years, they finally arrived at the promised land. Only God forbade Moses to enter because of an instance of disobedience. Moses' entire job was to get to the land God promised. Did Moses fail because he personally didn't set foot in the promised land? I'll bet those Israelites didn't think so. Here are just a few of Moses' amazing accomplishments along the way:

- Freed Israelites from slavery
- Divided the Red Sea
- Wrote the Ten Commandments (with God's help)

- Led one million people in the desert for forty years
- Brought them to the promised land

Moses' many successes were not void because of one act of failure. That's because God uses circumstances we define as failures to achieve His purposes. When we decide to follow God and make Jesus the Lord of our lives, we submit ourselves to His purposes. We don't always understand how God works. Our God is in the heavens, and He does whatever He wants. Sometimes He takes a willing follower and places her into His divine plan for another person's good.

Author Verla Gillmor observed how God used Jesus for our good:

> Jesus' death on the cross looked like a failure. He hung there exposed and forsaken by his own Father. An angry mob called him a phony. He had warned his disciples that dark day was coming, telling them it would not be the end of the story. But when it happened, I doubt his followers believed any part of that could remotely "work for the good of anyone who loves him." Who knew?[1]

Another way God uses failure is to protect us from something we can't see. It might be God's hand on our shoulder before we step off a cliff. Your child might never know what could have happened. Injury? Temptation? Sin?

This manner of thinking is mature. It might be difficult for a young child to understand that God is working things out for his good and the good of another at the same time. As your child matures, this reason for failure makes sense. Choosing to believe God is working even failure out for our good helps ease the pain.

Acknowledge Failure as a Part of Life

In a magazine writing class I teach, I open with an invitation to consider all the fears about writing that people have. Normally these fears involve failure: failure to come up with a good idea, writing a bad article, having writer's block, and rejection by an editor. Whereas in most areas of life, 90 percent of our fears don't come true, I believe that in writing 100 percent of our fears *will* come true. So if an author accepts that an editor will reject their work, she isn't devastated when it happens. Speakers are told to imagine that 10 percent of the people in every audience won't like their presentation. We can't please everyone.

Some people think when you acknowledge failure as an option, you have already doomed yourself to fail. I choose to practice realistic thinking and teach my children to do the same. Realistic thinking shrugs off failure as a part of life and a learning experience—not an end to a dream.

Until we get to heaven, we will fail at something, and perfectionistic thinking isn't healthy. It breeds anxiety and worry. Matthew 6:34 says, "Therefore do not worry about tomorrow, for tomorrow will worry about itself. Each day has enough trouble of its own." Give your child advance permission to make a mistake, have a bad day, fail a test, and sit the bench, and you'll have an emotionally healthier child.

Have Patience Until the Harvest

Galatians 6:7-8 says, "Do not be deceived: God cannot be mocked. A man reaps what he sows. The one who sows to please his sinful nature, from that nature will reap destruction; the one who sows to please the Spirit, from the Spirit will reap eternal life."

Paul used the analogy of planting to explain the principle of spiritual growth. He encouraged his readers to sow into the things of God with the promise they would reap the things of God. In the life of a Christian, we sow into God by how we think, speak, act, and spend our money and our time. These are investments in a God-honoring life, which reap a harvest of blessing.

What if we considered our children's hearts and lives a garden? The principles of sowing and reaping apply as well. Every day we sow into those "gardens" through our words, behavior, and the disciplines we teach them. However, just like a vegetable garden, if we plant carrot seeds, we will reap carrots—not corn. Consequently, if we sow negative seeds of discouragement, we will reap despair. If we sow seeds of impatience, we will reap frustration. If we sow seeds of laziness, we will reap stress.

Conversely, if we sow healthy seeds of good choices, we will reap self-discipline. If we sow seeds of patience, we will reap peace. If we sow seeds of perseverance, we will reap success. Our children's hearts are filled with rich soil that has been prepared by God to receive good seed. As conscientious gardeners, we need to plant good seed and reap a harvest for the kingdom of God.

What if you don't see results right away? That's normal. After a few days, the farmer doesn't get frustrated with slow growth and rip the seeds out of the ground. No. The farmer continues to water the soil, shoo the birds away, and pull the weeds. The farmer protects the seed until it has a chance to grow in its own time.

Taking the analogy one step further, perseverance is the seed, and failure is the weed in our children's lives. Weeds don't destroy good seeds, but they leach the nutrients out of the soil and limit the growth of the plant. Failure doesn't destroy our children's potential—it just sucks the enthusiasm from their hearts.

To overcome the pain and heartache of failure, children need a parent who will step in with fresh water and bright sunlight, while plucking the weed from the soil. With this tender care, perseverance and self-discipline will grow and develop. Then in time our children will produce a harvest of obedience and confidence and walk in victory—in God's timing and in His perfect will.

> This is love for God: to obey his commands. And his commands are not burdensome, for everyone born of God overcomes the world. This is the victory that has overcome the world, even our faith. Who is it that overcomes the world? Only he who believes that Jesus is the Son of God (1 John 5:3-5).

Memory Verses

*Jesus replied, "What is impossible with
men is possible with God."*

LUKE 18:27

*To him who is able to keep you from falling and to
present you before his glorious presence without fault and
with great joy—to the only God our Savior be glory,
majesty, power and authority, through Jesus Christ our
Lord, before all ages, now and forevermore! Amen.*

JUDE 1:24-25

*Though a righteous man falls seven times, he rises
again, but the wicked are brought down by calamity.*

PROVERBS 24:16

*Those who hope in the LORD will renew their strength.
They will soar on wings like eagles; they will run and
not grow weary, they will walk and not be faint.*

ISAIAH 40:31

*Being confident of this, that he who began
a good work in you will carry it on to
completion until the day of Christ Jesus.*

PHILIPPIANS 1:6

Encouraging Words

Develop success from failures. Discouragement and failure are two of the surest stepping stones to success.

—DALE CARNEGIE

If we did all the things we were capable of doing, we would literally astound ourselves.

—THOMAS EDISON

Adversity causes some men to break; others to break records.

—WILLIAM A. WARD

Go back a little to leap further.

—JOHN CLARKE

It is hard to fail, but it is worse never to have tried to succeed.

—THEODORE ROOSEVELT

Discussion or Journal Questions

1. Why is failure such a painful life experience?

2. When you have failed in the past, what have people done or said that was most helpful?

3. From God's perspective, what is true failure?

4. Have you ever labeled yourself with a negative name? Pick one of the names God calls you and write out that Scripture

on a note card. Then post that note card where you will see it every day.

5. How can we know God's will when we are facing a decision?

6. What types of positive past experiences make failure easier to overcome?

7. Why is perseverance such an important Christian virtue to teach our children?

8. Even when we succeed at our goals, what heart attitude can displease God?

9. Is there anything you've neglected to pray about—especially concerning your children and something they are trying to achieve? Commit now to pray about it.

10. What character virtue would you like to sow into your child's life? Write out a few ideas and commit to sow seeds of that virtue into your child.

Chapter Eight

Body Awareness

Jack Sprat could eat no fat...

I grew up a freckle-faced, hazel-eyed brunette in a neighborhood of blonds—thirteen of them. Lori, Trisha, Andrea, and Johnny, to name a few. Even my sister was blond. Not just any kind of blond, but the light, almost white, kind of blond. With their light hair and blue eyes, they could have all been part of the same family. Only one child stood out in the crowd. Me.

I was very aware of the difference. Because this was before the days of Sun-In, there wasn't much I could do. Normally my brown hair didn't matter to my friends, except when we played "Big Valley."

In the mid to late sixties, *The Big Valley* was a popular television show. For those of you over 40, I can almost hear you humming the theme song right now. As little kids we would reenact the various episodes, and inevitably there would be an argument over who would get to play Audra Barkley.

Audra was the beautiful, long-haired daughter, whose mama fussed over her and three handsome brothers pampered her. As much as I would have liked to play Audra, that was never an option. You see, Audra had long, *blond* hair. With my brown hair, no one considered me for the part of Audra. All I could do was stand back and let the other girls argue over who would play Audra that day.

Thankfully I did get a part to play. I was Nick. Yes, you read that correctly. Nick. For those not familiar with the television show, Nick was the hot-tempered, dark-haired, middle son who ran the ranch.

I would have rather played Heath, the handsome younger brother played by Lee Majors. But the one blond boy in the neighborhood got to play blond Heath.

When I didn't play Nick, I played a horse. I wish I were kidding, but it is true. That's what happens when you are a tall child. You are too big to ride on someone else's back. I can still feel the pebbles pressing into my knees to this day.

Although I share a somewhat humorous story to begin this chapter, the truth is it hurts to be labeled and categorized based on something we can't help, but it happens every day. Children are especially hurtful to each other in the area of appearance. As they struggle to find their own place in their little social hierarchies, it's as if their internal radars zero in on anything different from the norm—whatever normal happens to be in that setting. Every part of another child's body can become a target of ridicule: color of skin, height, weight, hair color, size of ears, glasses, a scar, or braces.

Children's words become weapons. *Move over, fatty! Hey, four-eyes! String bean!* Those words hang in the air for a fraction of a second until they are absorbed into the heart of the listener. Shame sets in. Embarrassment. Hiding. Lies become truth in the soul of a child.

Most kids find it easier to laugh at the jeers, while a few with a warrior spirit learn to retaliate with words or fists. Tears often come later when no one is looking. No matter the response, all kids carry those negative labels deep in their hearts, ready to be resurrected at a moment's notice.

There will always be people telling our children how they should look—both directly and indirectly. Even if no one speaks a word, children compare and contrast themselves with others consciously and unconsciously. Can parents counteract the constant bombardment of the world's image of beauty with the truth? Absolutely! It will be a challenge, but armed with the truth of God, it is possible.

The "Perfect Body" Myth

Our children view media images of "perfection" at an earlier age than any other generation in history. Many experts believe that the media has unknowingly triggered a backlash of low self-esteem in many children and adults. The images of physical beauty and bodily perfection splash across television, movies, and magazine covers, demonstrating to even the youngest children what they are *not*.

Our obsession with looks is so severe that Remuda Ranch, an internationally-respected Christian recovery program for eating disorders, reports that approximately one out of three American women and 15 percent of men will have an eating disorder or related problem at some time in their lives.[1] It's impossible to point to one cause of this problem. The experts at Remuda Ranch offer several reasons, "Many factors contribute to the development of an eating disorder, such as peer pressure, perfectionism, trauma, low self esteem, and certainly the influence of media in today's culture."[2]

As parents we have an obligation to infuse our children with the truth about their value and inner beauty, which is totally separate from our physical bodies. In fact our physical bodies are only the vehicle God uses to house our spiritual nature. Our bodies will only be around for 70 to 90 years, but our spirits will live eternally.

The apostle Paul conveyed this truth to the Christians in Corinth when they faced hardships, including possible death for their faith, "That is why we never give up. Though our bodies are dying, our spirits are being renewed every day" (2 Corinthians 4:16 NLT). Although we give honor and value to our bodies as the temples of the Holy Spirit (1 Corinthians 6:19), they should not be our source of confidence or the definition of our value.

Jesus said, "If you hold to my teaching, you are really my disciples. Then you will know the truth, and the truth will set you free" (John 8:31-32). The only truth that sets us free is the truth we *know*. If our children don't *know* the truth about their value, the myth of a perfect body will hold them in bondage.

Colossians 2:8 confirms the importance of the truth, "See to it that no one takes you captive through hollow and deceptive philosophy, which depends on human tradition and the basic principles of this world rather than on Christ." The world is feeding our children a diet of "hollow and deceptive philosophy." It's up to us to direct them to the truth.

Focus on the Truth

Jennifer was an active, intelligent, and outgoing child. She made friends easily and excelled in academics. First and second grade slipped by without incident. Jennifer loved school and found joy in being around friends. Everything was happily uneventful until third grade. That's when the difference in Jennifer's appearance became an issue.

One day she came home with the heartbreaking news that some of the children were calling her "fat." Jennifer couldn't run as fast as the other kids and had trouble participating in some of the games on the playground. These athletic challenges prompted the name-calling, and Jennifer assumed her lack of skill was because of her weight. What hadn't been issues before—her weight and athletic challenges—were now painfully obvious to Jennifer.

The label of "fat" could have been devastating. At the tender age of eight, her physical development was just beginning, and negative comments could have heightened her sensitivity. Thankfully her mother and father, Jody and Bud, stepped in immediately with the truth.

The first truth was her athletic ability and weight were two different issues. Jody pointed out that Jennifer had never liked sports and, therefore, had never tried hard to achieve in that area. "Fat" was the label the other kids gave her, but the truth was that she was simply unathletic.

By identifying this truth, Jody and Bud were able to help Jennifer redirect her focus. Jody recalls, "What that situation made us do was focus on her natural strengths and not dwell on the things she couldn't do." Bud and Jody emphasized Jennifer's scholastic achievements, leadership ability, and social skills.

The second truth was that the unkind words of others didn't define Jennifer. The size of her body didn't define her either. Jody and Bud saw the importance of conveying to their daughter that God loved and accepted her for who she was, not what she looked like—and so did they. Just as important, Jennifer didn't have to make any changes for that love to continue. Jody said, "We could have fed her carrots and celery sticks and made her play sports, but we thought that would be more detrimental because it could have conveyed, 'We don't love you for who you are—we want you to be this way.' But then that would have just reinforced what she was already experiencing."

Jennifer's parents gave her a gift that year. They taught her the truth about herself. The name-calling tapered off in fourth grade, even though Jennifer's weight didn't change. Knowing the truth about her worth gave Jennifer the freedom to accept her differences and delight in how God made her.

Acknowledge Your Child's Assets

Even though our appearance shouldn't define us, our bodies have value because God created them. The Bible tells us that God was involved from the very beginning: "For you created my inmost being; you knit me together in my mother's womb" (Psalm 139:13). God created every part of us—our inner and outer being. One way God created us was with a need for love, which isn't surprising since the Bible tells us that God Himself is love (1 John 4:8).

Author William J. Richardson writes about this love-hunger in his book *Loving Obedience*. Richardson teaches the importance of meeting our children's need for love before we can ever address discipline issues. The first way to show love to our children, according to Richardson, is by acknowledging our child's physical attributes as a work of God and, therefore, worthy of our affirmation.

"Our children too are wonderful works of God with hundreds of thousands of assets. However, we lack the vision to see them. Our fallen world has trained us to miss the obvious," Richardson said.[3]

The truth is God created our children with an assortment of wonderful assets. These assets are qualities not acquired by effort but given by God. Richardson says that as we acknowledge assets, "We are actually teaching them the truth—they are the workmanship of God; His works are wonderful."

When describing assets, Richardson includes personality as well as physical characteristics. For the purpose of this chapter, we'll focus on the physical.

Richardson suggests parents should discover the assets, verbally label the assets, and verbally express pleasure or delight in the assets. I'll use my daughter Cathrine for an example. God chose Cathrine as my daughter from the continent of Africa and blessed her with strikingly beautiful facial features—particularly her full lips. Knowing that this could be a source of insecurity, I have intentionally affirmed this God-given attribute. I have said simple things like, "You have beautiful lips, and I love how full they are." I also tell her that some women spend lots of money for lips like hers.

Our son Dylan has lovely green eyes. I have made comments like, "Dylan, your eyes are such a cool shade of green. I really like them."

My father wasn't effusive with praise, but I can still picture myself standing in front of his chair as he counted the freckles on my face. "Let's see how many there are today!" he would say. Then with a smile on his face, he would touch the tip of his finger to my face and begin to count. My father's enjoyment of my freckles was like a protective covering for any unkind comments directed my way. My sun-kissed face was never an embarrassment to me. While the other girls spread lemon juice on their cheeks to fade the brown spots, I was content.

My youngest son has my coloring, and I've applied my father's legacy to him. However, I elect to suggest that perhaps his freckles are places where angels kissed him. Then I place my finger on his tanned cheeks and begin the count.

For an easy and enjoyable exercise, make a list of your child's many assets. Think of your child from head to toe and identify his or her physical characteristics. Then plan to address them one by one at different times in the coming weeks.

Paint a Word Picture

I grew up around my father's mother, Grandma Owens. She was a little Welsh lady who let my little sister and me sell mud pies to her neighbors, snuggle next to her in her bed at night, and made us macaroni and cheese from scratch. Grandma always had braces on her legs and was limited in her walking ability, so our activities were quiet ones. I have many delightful memories of my grandma, but one sticks out in my mind. She used to call me her little black-eyed Susan. Although I was one of many grandchildren, I remember being loved by my grandmother with unconditional love. This pet name affirmed her love in a way I can't explain.

Something in my child's heart warmed as my grandmother compared me to a beautiful flower and showed me her pleasure. Although I don't completely understand the power of a word picture, to me it was an effective way to communicate love and approval—especially because my sister had the more traditionally beautiful blond hair and blue eyes.

Using a Metaphor

Jesus understood the power of a word picture and used it effectively. In writing we call it a metaphor; using one thing to describe another. Jesus' most powerful metaphors were used to describe Himself:

- Bread of life (John 6:35)
- Light of the world (John 8:12)
- Gate (John 10:9)
- Vine (John 15:5)

Metaphors create a strong and memorable picture in the mind of the hearer or reader. They did this for Jesus' followers then and now. We can use this same power of a metaphor with our children, providing it is uplifting. Many parents do this naturally with nicknames, although not always with the best results. After all, who wants to be compared to a pumpkin? Nicknames like "Tiger" or "Princess" create much more positive associations.

Having three naturally competitive boys challenged me to be creative in how I encouraged their individual strengths. As their parents, my husband and I delighted in the differences between the three of them. They didn't always see it that way. When they compared themselves to each other in athletics and academics, they noticed their weaknesses more than their strengths. To help them feel better about their strengths, we compared them to an animal that shared a similar strength. Josh is solid and strong, and he became our lion. Robbie is thin and nimble, and he became a cheetah. Dylan is fast and savvy, and so he was our jaguar.

The boys loved the comparison to a beautiful animal. While these didn't become nicknames, we were able to affirm their unique physical abilities using words that carried great meaning.

What image reminds you of your child? Does your daughter remind you of a rose with her pink cheeks? Does your son remind you of a race car when he runs fast? Does your teenager remind you of a willow tree when she dances? Paint a word picture using a metaphor that shows your delight in how God made them.

Using a Simile

Another use of powerful words is a simile. A simile compares one thing to another. For example, "she's as pretty as a picture" or, "he's as strong as an ox." The Bible uses similes to communicate human beauty. In Song of Solomon 4:1-2, we read the words of a husband to his beloved, "Your hair is like a flock of goats descending from Mount Gilead. Your teeth are like a flock of sheep just shorn…" While hearing that from my husband might not cause my heart to beat faster, it had great meaning in 1000 BC.

The New International Version of the Bible offers this explanation: "The beloved's black tresses flowing from her head remind the lover of a flock of sleek black goats streaming down one of the hills of Gilead."[4] And her teeth are clean and white like the sheep. Okay, now I get it.

I've used similes many times to affirm the God-given design of my children. I told Dylan that his wavy hair is like the sea. I love Robbie's straight hair too and tell him his hair is like strands of gold when the sun hits it.

When our daughters joined the family, Ruth (the youngest) immediately started talking about how much she loved white skin and how she wished she were white. I spoke the truth when I told her how her skin glistens when we put lotion on it, and how beautiful the color brown is, like hot chocolate. It's been years since she mentioned anything about her skin color, and she proudly slathers lotion on herself.

This is a fun way to affirm a child's assets in a vibrant way and create lasting memories.

Redirect to the Heart of the Matter

There is often a tendency to become overly concerned with our physical bodies. After all, we reside in a structure that needs constant attention. From cleansing, to feeding, to getting enough rest, maintaining our bodies is a full-time job. As important as our bodies are, we often find Jesus redirecting His disciple's attention away from physical demands and toward the things of God. One such example is found in Matthew 6:25-26,33:

> Therefore I tell you, do not worry about your life, what you will eat or drink; or about your body, what you will wear. Is not life more important than food, and the body more important than clothes? Look at the birds of the air; they do not sow or reap or store away in barns, and yet your heavenly Father feeds them. Are you not much more valuable than they?... But seek first his kingdom and his righteousness, and all these things will be given to you as well.

The disciples worried about the practical side of life. They weren't so different from us. The disciples wanted to talk about their bodies' needs, but Jesus wanted to redirect them to what really matters—seeking

God's kingdom and righteousness. God's kingdom is anywhere the rule and reign of God is—which should definitely be in our hearts.

Jesus was so passionate about caring for the heart rather than the outside appearance, that we find one of His strongest sermons on this topic in Matthew 23:27-28:

> Woe to you, teachers of the law and Pharisees, you hypocrites! You are like whitewashed tombs, which look beautiful on the outside but on the inside are full of dead men's bones and everything unclean. In the same way, on the outside you appear to people as righteous but on the inside you are full of hypocrisy and wickedness.

Although I grew up loving Jesus, I was much more concerned about how I looked on the outside than on the inside. And I obsessed more about my performance and accomplishments than how I looked. I neglected the condition of my heart until a move across country stripped me of all my achievements. When everything on the outside was gone, what remained was a selfish and bitter heart. I could have been a Pharisee.

Jesus was passionate about having a heart that was pure and reserved his harshest criticism for those who looked good on the outside but were spiritually dead on the inside. As our children grow up in a world that rewards outward success and beauty, it is our mandate to redirect them to consider the condition of their hearts.

Although we could teach this truth until we are blue in the face, author Ginger Plowman suggests a more effective way to teach a right heart-attitude, and that is to carefully draw out the thoughts of our children. In her book *Don't Make Me Count to Three*, Plowman observes, "When you help your child to understand what is in his heart, you are teaching him to evaluate his own motives, which will help to equip him for his walk with Christ as he grows into an adult."[5]

Instead of dealing with the surface issue first, Plowman suggests that parents become "heart-probers" and learn to help their children express what they are thinking and how they are feeling. Not only does this help a child move past issues in her life, but it helps her realize that God made her as more than just a physical being. She has a heart and soul that is worth pursuing.

Beware of Fixing the Problem

As my friend Jody shared the story about her daughter Jennifer's third grade experience, one question kept entering my head: Should Jody have helped her daughter lose weight? After all, wouldn't that have solved the problem? Admittedly I'm a fixer. I always need to rein myself in when someone shares a problem because before they are finished, my mind starts ticking off the possible solutions.

Being a journalist by training, I forced myself to ask the question I imagined many other parents would be asking: If you could do something about your child's physical condition, should you? Jody looked at me directly and said, "For Jennifer it was an emotional issue. We knew there was always going to be something people would comment about, so we turned it into what she could learn from it. Jennifer's self-esteem was much more important at that time in her life than her weight."

Those were words of wisdom I needed to hear. Losing weight would have been a shortsighted solution. Jody's solution to affirm Jennifer unconditionally was a long-term commitment to her daughter's sense of worth. Jennifer is now married, a professional educator, and a confident woman who loves and serves Jesus. Jody was right.

While there are definitely times to intervene, especially when a child's health is at risk, we need to be careful about our motives. If our motives are to change our children's looks based on what other people will think or say, we are driving down a dangerous path. This confirms a false truth to our child. If, however, we are making changes to improve their health, then the focus should be on that rather than appearance.

See Your Child As God Does

An artist visited a park every day to paint. He went when the lighting was perfect and stayed for hours, watching people walk by, looking for a face to paint. One day a raggedy beggar caught his eye. There was no attractive outward appearance to recommend this man to the painter. However, the artist knew God's handiwork was reflected in this man's heart. So he decided to paint the man as he imagined he could be.

Finally the artist completed his work and called the beggar over to see the painting. "Is that me?" the beggar asked.

"That is the 'you' God sees!" replied the artist.

The beggar looked at the painting, then looked at the artist. With tears running down his cheeks, he softly spoke, "If that's the man God sees, then that's the man I will be."

The artist looked beyond the outward appearance and captured the essence of the beggar through his painting. He saw beyond the unshaven chin, sunburned face, and ragged clothes to the man inside. As parents we can inspire our children to move beyond their appearance and become the man or woman God designed. In a world that is increasingly consumed with outward beauty that is fleeting and performance that will fade away, this is God's lasting answer and one of the greatest gifts we can give.

Author Carol Brazo summarized this issue brilliantly in her book *No Ordinary Home.* She wrote:

> If there were one biblical truth I wish I could give my children and lay hold of in my own deepest parts, it would be this one thing. He created me, He loves me, He will always love me. Nothing I do will change who I am. Being versus doing. The error was finally outlined in bold. I was always worried about what I was doing...God's only concern was and is what I am being—a child of His, forgiven, justified by the work of His Son, His heir...The only thing I need to do is come to grips with God's way of seeing me.[6]

May this truth saturate your mind and heart, so that when your child is frustrated with how God made him or her—how tall, short, light, dark, slow, fast, and so on—you can remind them God sees, God knows, and God loves no matter what...and so do you.

Memory Verses

For you created my inmost being; you knit me together in my mother's womb. I praise you because I am fearfully and wonderfully made; your works are wonderful, I know that full well.

PSALM 139:13-14

Don't be concerned about the outward beauty of fancy hairstyles, expensive jewelry, or beautiful clothes. You should clothe yourselves instead with the beauty that comes from within, the unfading beauty of a gentle and quiet spirit, which is so precious to God.

1 PETER 3:3-4 NLT

The LORD does not look at the things man looks at. Man looks at the outward appearance, but the LORD looks at the heart.

1 SAMUEL 16:7

Just as each of us has one body with many members, and these members do not all have the same function, so in Christ we who are many form one body, and each member belongs to all the others. We have different gifts, according to the grace given us.

ROMAN 12:4-6

Now you are the body of Christ, and each one of you is a part of it.

1 CORINTHIANS 12:27

Encouraging Words

All that glitters is not gold.

—Miguel de Cervantes

*The greatest single cause of a poor self-image
is the absence of unconditional love.*

—Zig Ziglar

*The Lord prefers common-looking people.
That is why he made so many of them.*

—Abraham Lincoln

Think not I am what I appear.

—Lord Byron

Discussion or Journal Questions

1. We bring glory to God when we affirm how He has created us. How has God made you unique? List some of your talents, interests, spiritual gifts, or personal characteristics.

2. Does considering your body as the handiwork of God change how you feel about it? Should it? Why or why not?

3. Read 1 Samuel 16:7. Why would God create us with a body, then say He's looking past it?

4. What are the dangers of ignoring the conditions of our hearts?

5. In what way is inner beauty revealed in the life of a follower of Christ? How is it manifest in everyday life?

6. What can happen if we try to fix an area of our physical bodies with the wrong motive?

7. Although we may accept the truth that our looks don't matter as much as our character, why is this difficult to accept in our hearts?

8. What benefits would your child receive from having you help him examine his heart?

9. List some of the benefits in your family, workplace, and church if people looked past the appearances of others and looked at their hearts.

Chapter Nine

Hope After Loss: Dealing with Grief

Little Bo Peep has lost her sheep…

My husband, children, and I traded the oppressive desert heat for the cool breezes of the mountains over the Fourth of July weekend in 2004. We packed our tent trailer and headed east for five days of playing in the woods, fishing, and s'mores around the campfire. We also spent those five days with no cell phone contact. It was a wonderful break.

On our way home, when we arrived in the town closest to the campground, I turned on my cell phone to touch base with my mother back in the valley. As my phone took a minute to warm up and locate service, I enjoyed my last views of the aspens and pine trees. Before I could dial, however, my phone beeped, alerting me that I had a message. Five in fact. I dialed my answering service and prepared to hear normal messages from friends who hadn't realized we were away. But that's not what I heard.

The first message stole the breath from my lungs and turned the pit of my stomach to cold dread. It was my older sister Paula, barely able to utter the words between great gasping sobs: "Glynnis…come…home." That's all she got out before that message ended.

Without knowing what happened, the panic started my heart pounding. "Tod, something horrible has happened," I gasped.

Just then the second message started, and it was Paula's husband, David. His voice was much more self-controlled, and in words that erased all hope that the problem was minor, David told me very calmly that my niece Christa (Paula's and his daughter) had been killed in a car accident on the Fourth of July and asked if I could get home right away.

I sat in stunned silence for a second and then began to hyperventilate. I couldn't breathe. I barely heard my husband asking, "What happened? What happened?" but I couldn't answer him. It was like a nightmare and you have to get away from a monster, but your legs are like concrete blocks. No words would form. The only sound was me gasping for air.

He pulled off the road, got out of the car, and ran around to my side to see if he could help. I was able to calm down enough to tell him the devastating news, and he just held me while I sobbed.

Our three boys, ages 13, 11, and 9, sat in the backseat in shocked silence. Then the questions started. "Is it true? Did you misunderstand the message? What happened?" I had no answer to the last question and wished I could have told them it wasn't true. But the other three messages confirmed the truth. We had lost a loved one.

The next three hours of driving were painful. I was able to talk to my family but didn't want to hear any more of the story until I was sitting with my arms around my sister. We made it home safely, and the next few days were spent planning the funeral and hosting out-of-state family.

Our loss was sudden and devastating. Christa was full of life and brought joy into all our lives. She had recently recommitted her life to Christ, and the love of Jesus made her already loving presence even more pleasurable. She cared for and served her parents, grandmother, sisters, and aunts with a generosity seldom seen.

Not only did the adults struggle with Christa's death, but we had children of all ages who had to deal with the grief of losing a loved one. Christa loved children and invested her life into the lives of her young cousins and her sister Amy's twin boys, Gavin and Ronin. Christa basically moved in with Amy after the premature birth of the babies and then moved from California to Arizona to help raise them. The boys were four years old when they lost their beloved aunt.

In the midst of our own grief and sadness, we had children to care for and help deal with their own sadness. Because of the range of their ages, each one dealt with the loss of Christa differently. The fact is we didn't do everything right. We did the best we could do, given the circumstances, because none of us was prepared for this. We hadn't taken any classes in college, read any book, or studied how other families dealt with grief. In addition to being unprepared, we were handicapped by our own emotions.

Yes, we were devastated. But we weren't without hope because we grew up with a Christian mother and grandmother who taught us early on that there is more to life than what we see on earth. We know that Christa accepted Jesus as her Savior, and we look forward to the day when we will be reunited in a place where there is no more sorrow and no more tears.

Through the grace of God, we sought and received comfort after the loss of Christa. God helped us walk through the dark days following her death, renewed our hope, and gave us words to say to the children. They didn't grieve like we did, and we learned to take our lead from them in how to help them best. Although those were times I never want to repeat, I can now say with confidence and personal experience, that we serve a God who heals the brokenhearted—no matter how young or old.

Although children will grieve over a variety of losses, in this chapter we will focus on the loss of a loved one, whether a person or an animal. However, the principles of dealing with grief can apply to any type of loss.

Grief Is Grief

Grief is obvious in adults but harder to detect in children. Nevertheless, children can grieve just as deeply when faced with a significant loss. Children also grieve over events that adults deal with more easily, such as the move of a friend or a change in schools.

Acknowledging the reality of the pain is the first helping step. It may not look like an adult's grief, but it is real to the child. Well-meaning adults try to gloss over or hurry past the pain in a grieving child's life to minimize the sadness. While grief is always an unwelcome guest in our hearts, it must take its own course in order for there to be healing and wholeness on the other side.

As most adults know, there is no shortcut to getting over heartache. God's tender mercy and time are a healing combination. Accepting pain as a natural part of life will help a child deal with the sadness she will face as she grows. The truth is, if God grants us many years to live, we will experience pain and loss. That's just part of being a member of the human family.

By identifying common patterns of grieving in children, parents can be more aware of what's happening in the heart of a child and create opportunities to process the grief.

Children Grieve Differently than Adults

Young children relate to their world in concrete ways. Their minds don't comprehend intangible issues, such as time, life, and death. They can't grasp the concept of someone never coming back. When a young child experiences a loss, he doesn't fully understand the reality of the situation.

This doesn't mean young children are immune to grief. The reactions of those around them profoundly affect children, and they will respond to the fact that something is wrong.

Marlo Francis, author of *The Unkind Companion: Learning to Live with Loss,* has observed the following behaviors in small children:

> If they are very little, they will become more clingy and fussy—not easily consoled or calmed. Their normal schedules often are disrupted, and they react in a very "high maintenance" way. If they are in the three- to four-year range, their behaviors can become hostile, rambunctious, disrespectful, and boundary-testing. They might not even understand themselves why they are acting out...but it is because somewhere deep down, they feel their under-girding threatened—their stability rocked.[1]

By ages five to seven, most children are already wondering about death and will often ask very direct questions about what happens after someone dies and if it hurts, even before they have lost anyone. These questions might even be a result of their own deep fear over losing someone they love. So when they experience death, their grieving is more open and directly related to the loss. Children in this age group also watch the adults in their lives and look for cues on how to react. Hence, it is very important for the adults to model healthy grieving to children in this age range. This might involve the adults getting professional help if needed.

Children between the ages of eight and twelve react very differently than the early elementary age range. They vacillate between experiencing the feelings of a small child and feeling the need to act like an adult. As a result, they might hide emotions they label in their own heads as "childish." Forcing a child to talk it out probably won't help. Parents can help their children by spending time together doing normal activities. The normalcy will bring comfort to a child and will help create a setting in which the child feels safe enough to share her feelings.

By the time a child reaches the teenage years, he reasons much like an adult—but not exactly. As parents of teenagers know, there is often a spirit of invincibility. This becomes very concerning especially once the teenager starts driving or participates in any adventurous sports. A teenager should be allowed time and space to process the loss in his or her own way.

Trauma Residue

One consistent thread Marlo has noticed running throughout all age ranges is the tendency for "trauma residue," as she calls it. When a child loses someone to death, she can manifest behaviors similar to those seen in obsessive-compulsive disorders. These behaviors might be short-lived but, if not dealt with properly, can be permanent.

Marlo observes, "It seems that the insecurity death leaves behind can plant seeds in little ones that make them want to control their environment so that nothing ever hurts them or pulls the rug out from underneath them again. No surprises. For my son, it took almost a year for him not to obsess over little things like who was picking him up from school, if he had enough lunch money, what we were doing every night and so on. He didn't even realize why he was doing it—but in essence, he wanted to always feel as if he knew the game plan."

Creating a dependable routine can help children feel secure at times like this. Increase your communication regarding everyday things even though it may seem repetitive or unnecessary. Print out a weekly schedule and post it on the refrigerator. Allow your child to have his own daily planner, if that would help.

Be sensitive to unusual concerns your child expresses and take small steps to bring comfort to your child. Simple things, such as printing out phone numbers and putting them in a backpack, might be all your child needs to feel secure.

Be Honest with Discretion

One of the least helpful things a parent can do when a child is grieving is to make up answers to hard questions to ease a child's pain. Although there might be temporary comfort in an easy answer, it creates more long-term questions and confusion.

Children do not need to know all the details, but they deserve the truth at their level of understanding. When my niece was killed, all we told the youngest children was that Christa had been hurt in an accident, and she was hurt so badly that she died. They did not need to know any other details. The older children were told she was a victim in a drunk driving accident, but they were spared any other details about the accident.

A child's personality also determines how much he or she should know. In our family, one of my children is sensitive. While his siblings could laugh off a scary part of a movie, he would remember the details and worry and fret for days. He was on a need-to-know basis for years. He is now an early teenager and is able to deal with much more. For sensitive children, guard your conversations about the loss.

As you discuss the loss and any of the events, such as the funeral and burial, allow your child to ask any question. Emphasize that every question is important and welcome. This will open up opportunities for honest communication that will help move the healing process along. Answer simply and with discretion.

When There's No Easy Answer

When Jennifer was six years old, her parents gave her a kitten for her birthday. Jennifer loved that cat and carried it everywhere. She dressed it up like a baby doll, and the two slept together every night. It was the perfect cat for a little girl, and they were inseparable. When it came time to get the cat spayed, Jennifer was very worried about the possible consequences and wanted to know all the details. So Jody, her mom, talked to her about the surgery and even took her to see the veterinarian.

The vet was very caring, and he took Jody and Jennifer on a tour of the hospital, showing them every step of the process. They set the surgery appointment and went home. Although her daughter is now grown, Jody remembers that time clearly. "We prayed every day for the next two weeks for the surgery, and I kept assuring Jennifer that it would be okay. I kept telling her she could trust God with everything in her life, including her cat."

The morning of the surgery arrived, and Jennifer went to school late so she could go with her mom to the vet, kiss the cat goodbye, and talk to the vet one more time. The surgery was successful, but something went horribly wrong in the recovery process. At 1:30 in the afternoon, Jody received a call saying the cat was dead after a freak accident.

That day the vet followed the normal procedure for performing surgery on the animals and then allowed them to rest in a warming room after surgery. All the animals went into that room. At that time there were three cats and three dogs. The last animal brought in was a black Labrador retriever. When they brought the Lab in, it immediately came out of anesthesia and attacked all three of the cats.

When Jody picked up Jennifer from school, their plan was to go straight to the vet. Instead, Jody had to deliver news that would devastate her daughter. Jody remembers thinking, *How am I going to defend you, God?*

Jody took her daughter home, and together they cried and prayed. Jody realized that letting her daughter grieve and not trying to solve the problem helped the most. Jody said, "We didn't try to offer an explanation, and that was probably the most healing to her."

There were no easy answers to the questions running through Jennifer's mind. At the top of the list was why would God allow this to happen, especially after Jennifer had prayed for the protection of her precious cat. Jody knew she couldn't answer for God, and she didn't try to. Because Jody had lived out her faith in God, Jennifer knew that in spite of this horrible event, God was still good.

Life will often present questions we can't answer. In spite of bad things that happen, we can reaffirm the goodness of God. Faith is believing things we can't always prove in the natural. Settling this issue in our hearts now and making a decision to trust God whatever happens help us model faith when questions arise that have no answers.

Joyce Meyers writes, "Trust will always require us to accept unanswered questions! We want answers to everything, but we must come to the place where we're satisfied to know the One who knows and place our trust in Him."[2]

The Question of Heaven

One of the biggest questions children have concerning death is the question of heaven. Children who have learned about the wonders of heaven will want to know if their loved one who has died is there. Unless you know for sure that the person proclaimed a faith in Jesus as their Savior, don't offer any guarantees to the child. Conversely don't tell a child that a person *isn't* in heaven. It is not up to us to judge the heart of another, and we walk on dangerous ground when we try to do that. My own father accepted Jesus on his deathbed at the invitation of my son Dylan, who was 12 at the time. An honest answer is that only God knows the heart of an individual.

However, when we know that our loved one accepted Jesus, then it is cause for celebration. Not a celebration that masks the grief, but a healthy acknowledgment that our loved one is experiencing the ultimate joy. As 1 Thessalonians 4:13 says, "Brothers, we do not want you to be ignorant about those who fall asleep, or to grieve like the rest of men, who have no hope." We do have hope, which lessens our grief.

The question of heaven can be a teachable moment with our children, not something to avoid. As Christians we have the hope of eternal life through Jesus Christ. In a very thoughtful and gentle way, this can be a time to explain how God wants everyone to live with Him forever in heaven. However, because God is perfect and holy, heaven is a place that is perfect too. Unfortunately God can't allow our sin (our wrong thoughts, actions, and words) in heaven. So God sent Jesus to forgive us our sins. All we have to do is accept Jesus' forgiveness and choose to follow Jesus here on earth.

Older children will understand that everyone is going to live forever somewhere. Now is the time to decide if it will be with God or apart from God. By making this decision, you can assure your child he will one day be in heaven too. This is a glorious promise in Scripture and one we can be confidently teaching our children. Knowing we will be reunited with other loved ones is a great comfort when we are grieving.

A Caution Against Overindulgence

When a child is grieving, it is natural to want to treat her to special meals, change sleeping or TV habits, take her on special trips, or buy her gifts. We want to make our child happy and hope that, for even a short moment in time, we can ease the pain. This is right and good for a while. However, there is the possibility that well-meaning parents and family members can overindulge a child.

Marlo Francis's son Ben was five when his father and grandfather died in a plane crash. It was a horrific way to lose two very beloved men. Following the accident, it was everyone's natural instinct to indulge Ben and do anything to make him happy or get his mind off his loss. However, after a time his mother realized Ben expected the special treatment. She spoke with a counselor about it, and he offered advice that was just what Ben needed.

The counselor told Marlo that children are more resilient than adults. The best thing she could do for Ben was to talk with him every day and let him know there was nothing he couldn't ask. Regarding the special treats, the counselor advised Marlo to keep the boundary lines identical to where they were before her husband died. If Ben couldn't have ice cream before dinner prior the plane crash, then he shouldn't have it now.

While special treatment shows great love and affection and can be very helpful, there is an even greater need for a child to find a new normal. Returning to regular routines and rules as quickly as possible actually helps stabilize a child. Marlo learned that children need to understand you can't indulge pain forever. The wound has to heal before the pain will cease.

Remember

Many children are afraid of death. Some may not want to go to the funeral or visit the gravesite. To an adult these seem like ways to honor the memory of a loved one and the right thing to do, but to a child, they may be very scary events. Whenever possible don't force a child to do something that scares him.

One way to replace sad memories with happy ones is to remember the good times with the loved one. As a family we went through old photos of Christa and made a video. On the first anniversary of her death, we took a family trip to the beach because she loved water. One night on that trip, we sat around a fire pit and shared funny stories about her. Even the children shared memories.

The fear of forgetting a loved one can be strong. Some families put together a memory book with letters and photos from friends. If your child is old enough to write, consider inviting her to write down some of her own memories. Other ways to remember might include lighting a candle, saying prayers, or writing a letter to the one who has passed away. There should be freedom with healthy limits when processing grief. As we discovered, if it helped and it was honoring to Christa and God, it was good.

Know Where Your Hope Is Found

I mentioned Marlo Francis several times in this chapter because she has traveled down this road of grief, rediscovered joy, and now ministers to others who are walking that same path. Even in the midst of her grief, Marlo was very aware of the importance of helping her son cope. Instead of crushing Marlo and Ben, God brought healing to both of them.

According to Marlo, one of the most important ways a parent can help a child through the grief process is to have a relationship with the Lord that is already firmly established. When loss entered her household, her foundation of hope was already established.

"Thankfully my relationship with the Lord was seasoned with time and passion, and when the moment came to draw from those resources, they were there in full supply," Marlo said. "This allowed me to wake each morning with hope. Ben picked up on that hope, and it was contagious, leading to the things that brought true healing into our lives."

GriefShare, a national Christian organization that ministers to the grieving, also believes that a relationship with Jesus is central to recovering from a loss. Here's why. If I center my life around another human being, then life will be shaken irreparably when that person leaves my life. But if my life is centered around Jesus, who will never leave me, then I have a firm foundation that can withstand the inevitable losses in my life.

Even children can know this confidence. As we introduce them to the Friend who will never leave them, Someone closer than a brother, a heavenly Father who never disappoints, and a Savior who always forgives, we are helping to establish a foundation in their lives that cannot be shaken.

Memory Verses

The LORD is close to the brokenhearted and
saves those who are crushed in spirit.

PSALM 34:18

There is a time for everything, and a season
for every activity under heaven.

ECCLESIASTES 3:1

Now is your time of grief, but I will see you again and
you will rejoice, and no one will take away your joy.

JOHN 16:22

Come to me, all you who are weary and burdened,
and I will give you rest. Take my yoke upon you
and learn from me, for I am gentle and humble
in heart, and you will find rest for your souls.

MATTHEW 11:28-29

We wait in hope for the LORD; he is our
help and our shield. In him our hearts
rejoice, for we trust in his holy name.

PSALM 33:20-21

Those who hope in the LORD will renew their strength.
They will soar on wings like eagles; they will run and
not grow weary, they will walk and not be faint.

ISAIAH 40:31

Encouraging Words

The pain passes, but the beauty remains.
—PIERRE AUGUSTE RENOIR

Friendship doubles our joy and divides our grief.
—SWEDISH PROVERB

We acquire the strength we have overcome.
—RALPH WALDO EMERSON

*We must meet the uncertainties of this world
with the certainty of the world to come.*
—A.W. TOZER

*Seeing death as the end of life is like seeing
the horizon as the end of the ocean.*
—DAVID SEARLS

Discussion or Journal Questions

1. In Matthew 5:4, we read the words of Jesus, "Blessed are those who mourn, for they will be comforted." What kinds of blessings come to a person who honestly mourns?

2. When you have mourned in the past, what brought you the most comfort?

3. People take very different lengths of time to grieve. Why do you think there is this difference between people?

4. Well-meaning people try to ease our grief, and it can often

come across in the wrong way. What are some wrong ways to offer comfort?

5. Do you think our culture has an impact on the way people grieve? If so, what would that be?

6. Grief includes other emotions like anger, regret, and bitterness. What are some healthy ways to process those other emotions?

7. What are the greatest problems in your life?

8. Sometimes problems cause us a form of grief, and we get stuck in a holding pattern. How can we grow spiritually when we are in a dark time of life?

9. If you are in a holding pattern, list three reasons to be thankful in the midst of your current situation.

10. Do you feel separated from God now? Take some time to examine your relationship with Him and write your thoughts here.

Chapter Ten

Anger: When Is It Wrong?

Mary, Mary quite contrary...

My little sister Lizzie and I were good friends growing up. She was a great companion and a willing participant in my plans. Lizzie joined the clubs I started, acted in my plays, and listened to me pretend I was a singer on the radio. We got along great except when we played a certain board game—Monopoly.

We always started out joyfully, moving our iron or shoe markers, buying up properties, and laughing good-naturedly when the other went to jail. Somewhere along the way, the camaraderie evaporated, and the game became less fun. Whether it started when one refused to sell a property or the other put too many houses on Indiana Avenue, I don't remember. What I do remember is how every game of Monopoly ended at our house: We threw the cards at each other and stalked off furious. We never finished a game—ever.

Knowing our personalities, I must confess that I probably started most of the fights. A typical firstborn, I liked things my way and probably pushed my easygoing sister too far. The strange thing is we did this many times. Perhaps in our youthful optimism, we thought we could handle the competition.

If you have more than one child in your home, you've probably experienced a similar situation. Simple things spark sibling anger. The very act of living in close daily contact with others causes irritations that can build up over time. You don't have to have an anger problem to have a problem with anger. Unfortunately it's part of our human natures—natures that need taming at times.

Most of the anger children and parents experience doesn't fall into the category of effective anger. Frustration and a desire to have one's own way normally drive anger. According to Tim LaHaye, author of *Spirit-Controlled Temperament*, "Anger is one of two universal sins of mankind. After counseling thousands of people, I have concluded that all emotional tension can be traced to one of two things—anger or fear. And sometimes the two are intertwined."[1]

Christians differ in their opinions on expressing anger. We read Scriptures like, "In your anger do not sin" from Ephesians 4:26, and we interpret it to mean that the emotion of anger is wrong. On the other hand, in three of the Gospels, we read about Jesus' response to people who misused God's temple for profit. John paints a particularly vivid picture of Jesus' response: "So he made a whip out of cords, and drove all from the temple area, both sheep and cattle; he scattered the coins of the money changers and overturned their tables. To those who sold doves he said, 'Get these out of here! How dare you turn my Father's house into a market!'" (John 2:15-16).

To help our children effectively deal with anger, we should spend some time considering the different aspects of this powerful emotion.

Responsible Versus Irresponsible Anger

Not all anger is sin. It couldn't be for two distinct reasons. First, Scripture tells us repeatedly in the Old Testament that God was angry. In Exodus 4:14, we read this verse: "Then the LORD's anger burned against Moses." Here's another example in Numbers 32:13: "The LORD's anger burned against Israel and he made them wander in the desert forty years, until the whole generation of those who had done evil in his sight was gone." The Israelites' disobedience made God angry.

Second, the New Testament records several examples of Jesus' anger. In Mark 3, Jesus entered the synagogue on the Sabbath and saw a man with a shriveled hand. Some Pharisees were there looking for reasons to accuse Jesus of doing wrong. Jesus, well aware of their intent, told the man with the shriveled hand to stand. Jesus spoke to the Pharisees, asking if it was lawful to do good and to give life on the Sabbath. Everyone remained silent. The Bible says, "He [Jesus] looked around at them in anger and, deeply distressed at their stubborn hearts, said to the man, 'Stretch out your hand.' He stretched it out, and his hand was completely restored" (Mark 3:5).

Jesus wasn't just tired and slightly annoyed. Scripture says our gentle Savior was angry. The Greek word used here is *orge*, which translates to "anger" and "agitation of the soul."[2] It also has the nuance of "anger exhibited in punishment." Scripture authors used this same word elsewhere, and it is translated more strongly into "wrath." Obviously this was more than a pet peeve.

There must be an appropriate form of anger because the Bible records that both God the Father and Jesus the Son were angry. Dan Russ, author of *Flesh-and-Blood Jesus*, observes that Jesus always displayed effective anger: "He [Jesus] was most passionate, and anger was one of his many passions, but he was always angry with a redemptive purpose."[3]

Russ summarizes Jesus' anger into three categories: (1) frustration at those who failed to understand Him, His calling, and teaching; (2) the harnessed anger of a teacher who captures the attention of His students with passion; and (3) righteous indignation at those who rejected God, God's truth, and those God loves. We find this type of anger in the example of Jesus in the temple mentioned earlier.

God did not exhibit this anger with selfish or malicious intent. Instead, it flowed out of a heart of love and the highest respect for people, truth, and holiness. Herein we find the difference between most of the anger displayed in our homes.

Marriage and Family therapist Les Carter calls this the difference between assertive and aggressive anger. Assertive anger can actually be motivating. Russ observes, "When used correctly, assertiveness is a positive trait. Certainly, each person faces many situations that go against his most basic beliefs. By being assertive, he demonstrates a sense of strong commitment to what he knows is right."[4]

Aggressive anger goes too far. Carter writes, "Like assertiveness, aggressive anger seeks to put forward one's beliefs about what one believes to be right. However, aggressive anger is used in an abrasive, insensitive way." Here's an example of the difference: Aggressive anger seeks to punish a person who does wrong. Assertive anger seeks to help a person who does wrong.

Given the many biblical examples of positive anger, we should be careful as parents not to condemn all anger. Our children may do great and mighty things for the kingdom of God while motivated by healthy anger at sin and things that grieve the heart of God. However, we should identify destructive anger and teach our children practical tools for identifying the source and managing it. For ease of writing and understanding, when I refer to anger throughout the rest of this chapter, it will be the destructive type.

Where Negative Anger Comes From

Luke 6:45 tells us, "The good man brings good things out of the good stored up in his heart, and the evil man brings evil things out of the evil stored up in his heart. For out of the overflow of his heart his mouth speaks." Anger doesn't manifest itself because of the actions of others. Anger arises from a heart that is not fully submitted to God and from the innate sinfulness therein.

Dr. Tim LaHaye offers this summary of the source of anger, "Stripped of all the façade and fancy excuses for condoning anger, of calling it 'Old Nick' or 'my natural Irish disposition,' we are confronted with an ugly word—selfishness…When I am angry, it is because someone has violated my rights, and I am interested in myself."[5]

It's not surprising that our hearts would be the source of trouble. One reason we have trouble dealing with sinful desires that come out of the heart is our misunderstanding of the word *heart* as used in a biblical context. When the readers of Luke's Gospel read the previously mentioned passage in chapter 6, they didn't have all the romantic images the word *heart* conveys today. They understood their hearts to be much more than an emotions factory and out of their control. To them it was the seat of their thinking, their feeling, and their choosing. It was the center of their soul, an all-encompassing part of their being.

By understanding God's design for our hearts, we realize we are not victims of out-of-control emotions. Our will and our emotions are connected. Hence, through the power of God, we can choose how we respond to difficult people or situations.

Anger comes from a choice to store up resentment, selfishness, unforgiveness, and bitterness. Unfortunately we don't always know we are doing this. It is possible that too many people have stored up evil in their hearts without knowing it. Then, when they least expect it, it overflows into the lives of others, causing broken relationships and broken emotions. For this reason we can save our children much pain by helping them deal with anger and its root causes before they lose friends, jobs, or worse, end up in divorce court.

Are There Contributing Factors?

Knowing my personality is melancholy and choleric (organized and in control), I prefer to have things in order. The times I get most frustrated and angry are when I can't find something that I need— especially when I know it was nearby a short while earlier. Normally I know exactly why I'm mad, and the good news is I can easily solve the problem by creating a designated place for everything. I've reduced frustration by having a key hook and specific places for the kids' homework, my purse, my husband's wallet, my watch, and so on.

Disorganization was a contributing factor to my anger, and the anger disappeared when I identified and solved the problem. As we evaluate the reasons for our children's anger, it's very likely there's an answer we can identify with some detective work.

There are many reasons why our children experience anger. Here are two.

Physical Stress

Every parent of a baby or toddler dreads the "meltdown" stage. That's when a baby transforms from a cooing, adorable charmer into a screaming bundle of frustration. Normally this is due to exhaustion, hunger, or discomfort. At that moment there's no way to calm that upset baby except to meet his or her needs—as fast as possible!

As our children develop, they normally outgrow this behavior and handle it in more mature ways by vocalizing their needs. Yet children will act in childish ways far into the teenage years. So when our child expresses anger and frustration every day at 3:00 p.m. we would be wise to consider a physical reason because she might just need a snack, a nap, or quiet time.

Other physical issues that can cause irritation in children include blood sugar issues (such as hypoglycemia) and allergies. Karen L. Maudlin, a licensed clinical psychologist specializing in marriage and family therapy, writes about a mother who was frustrated with her son's anger. The mother had already identified a seasonal pattern to her son Jimmy's behavior, and when his teacher mentioned she'd noticed ADD tendencies in the fall and winter, the mother wanted to know more.

Jimmy's mother suspected there might be an underlying issue. Dr. Maudlin said, "She spoke with Jimmy's tutor who confirmed the fall/spring pattern of losing focus, while doing well in summer and winter. I recommended allergy testing, which identified severe allergies to mold, pollen, ragweed, and grass. Jimmy was put on allergy medication, and within two weeks, the anger and the ADD-like behaviors disappeared. Jimmy was a new student and son."[6]

If you suspect there might be a physical reason for your child's emotional response, consider keeping a journal to determine patterns. Another simple way is to make one change at a time and see if it makes a difference.

Lack of Skill Set

I was an adequate math student but loved words more than numbers at an early age. In college I discovered my brick wall when it came to math—chemistry. My concrete-thinking mind couldn't grasp the unseen concepts. Night after night I sat at the kitchen table struggling to make sense of protons and neutrons, only to slam my book shut in tears. Private tutoring, study groups, and a lab partner who was a chemistry professor's daughter didn't help. My brain shut down at a certain point. I was angry at myself for not being able to understand it and at everyone else for not being able to explain it to me. I knew that was irrational, but I was mad.

Sometimes our children are missing a specific skill needed to accomplish a task. They might hit their own brick wall when asked to organize their room, write a thank-you note to Grandma, or read. Children can't always communicate their frustration, and it manifests itself as anger.

If your child is continually angry about a specific thing, perhaps it's time for a one-on-one teachable moment. Maybe your child needs help to break down a big task into smaller bits. Before assuming it's a character issue, determine if there isn't another cause, which might be easier to address.

Sometimes, however, it's more of a challenge to determine the cause of anger. That's when the root goes deeper than a lack of ability or allergies and down to the heart.

Reaching the Heart of Your Child

Physician and counselor Michael R. Emlet writes, "The Bible's emphasis on the inward origin of anger suggests that helping angry children involves more than mere anger management techniques. To solve your child's anger problem, you must target the source of his anger: his heart."[7]

Moms and dads don't get a lot of parental training in heart issues. When most parents seek help, it's usually for an outward behavior issue. We've got a problem, and we want it stopped. However, for lasting change in our children's lives (and our lives for that matter), we must address the root of the issue, and that's found in the heart.

My friend Ginger Plowman started a ministry based on this very concept called Preparing the Way. Based on biblical truths, Ginger teaches parents that the heart is the foundation of behavior, and we do our children a disservice when we focus primarily on behavior. By focusing on behavior without a heart change, we have the potential to raise little Pharisees—looking great on the outside but spiritually dark on the inside.

The goal of addressing the heart issue according to Ginger is "to bring him to the sober assessment of himself as a sinner, to help him recognize his need for Christ, and to teach him to act, think, and be motivated as a Christian."[8]

To learn this skill, we need only look to Jesus for our example. Rather than just telling people right and wrong, Jesus often asked thought-provoking questions to help them evaluate themselves. The questions took the focus off the circumstances and onto the sin in their own hearts.

We find a good example of this in the story used earlier when Jesus faced the Pharisees in the synagogue. Instead of accusing them of hypocrisy and self-righteous piety, Jesus asked this question, "Which is lawful on the Sabbath: to do good or to do evil, to save life or to kill?" Jesus' question required them to consider their attitude, which He knew needed an adjustment. This same practice can help our children evaluate the situation of their hearts. Ginger shares an example in her book of heart-probing questions a parent can ask. I've paraphrased an example of sibling conflict to make it work with this chapter. The questions would be asked by the parent.

> What emotion were you feeling when you yelled at your brother and slammed the door in his face? (The child will probably answer, "anger.")
>
> What did your brother do to make you mad? (This allows your child to explain the situation.)
>
> Did yelling at your brother and slamming the door make things better or worse between the two of you? (Although the answer is obvious, it gets the child to speak the truth out loud.)
>
> Why was what your brother did wrong? (There are usually two guilty parties in every argument. This question acknowledges

that the child was sinned against. It would be helpful to have a biblical foundation for why it was wrong.)

Using the biblical reason for the wrong behavior, the parent could turn to the other child and ask something like, "Were you promoting peace by _____ to your brother?"

"Yes, son, your brother did sin against you, but in what other ways could you have responded?" (Here's where you can use Scripture passages to identify biblical ways to respond.)

The important part of this strategy is identifying biblical guidelines both for and against specific behaviors. To find out what the Bible has to say about specific behaviors, use a concordance and identify specific passages on issues such as anger, greed, or stealing.

To help parents in their mission to reach the heart of their child, Ginger has put together a handy quick reference resource called "Wise Words for Moms" to help identify patterns of disobedience. She also lists examples of Scripture passages to help address the heart issues. Visit www.GingerPlowman.com for more information and click on "Products."

Create a Safe Environment

Creating a place where children can safely express their anger is difficult for many parents, including me. If I'm completely honest, I'm not comfortable with my children's anger. I grew up in a calm home, where we didn't express anger very often. When someone did express anger, it seemed out of proportion to the offense—either too little or too much.

My husband, on the other hand, had a different experience. His family expressed anger in inappropriate ways. In building our household based on godly principles, we've struggled with finding a healthy balance. Our heart is to raise emotionally healthy children, and so we continue to work at this. But it's difficult.

We have found that an effective way for our kids to express their frustration and anger is in a meeting setting rather than in the heat of the moment. We identify a time to sit down and talk about a problem. That gives everyone time to cool down and think about their emotions before erupting.

James 1:19 gives us excellent guidelines for discussing concerns. "My dear brothers, take note of this: Everyone should be quick to listen, slow to speak and slow to become angry, for man's anger does not bring about the righteous life that God desires." Postponing a discussion gives you an opportunity to follow these godly guidelines and hopefully develop a more righteous life.

We've also found it helpful to set ground rules for respectful behavior in the meeting. We have very specific guidelines about using a respectful tone of voice, choosing words that aren't accusing, and not leaving in anger.

Here are a few of our guidelines:

- Avoid the words "always" and "never." These words exaggerate the problem and put someone on the defensive.

- Do not use mean language or call one another names.

- Keep to the topic at hand. Bringing up past offenses isn't helpful.

- Focus on feelings. This takes work because anger is often the easiest emotion to show, but it usually covers up other feelings, like insignificance or fear.

- Keep our voices at a reasonable level. In other words, no shouting.

- Listen without interrupting.

Children need to know that their thoughts, feelings, and opinions have value. They also need practice expressing those in positive ways rather than angry ways. Depending on the age of your children, you might want to develop a family contract about how to handle anger. Many children have a heightened sense of justice—it just gets mixed up with selfishness. We can allow them to explore this sense of justice and solve problems at the same time by creating a safe place to talk things over.

Preannounce Logical Consequences for Behavior

Often our children get angry over parental punishment that seems unfair. I might walk in from a hard day at work to find dirty dishes in the sink, shoes and socks thrown around the living room, the television left on, and kids nowhere in sight. This type of scenario would certainly elicit an unpleasant response from me. I would probably find the kids, set them down for an angry lecture, and assign a punishment that arose from my frustration. The kids would be angry too, and there would be an argument. This argument would increase in fervor if the kids thought the punishment was unfair.

One way to reduce anger from these common confrontations is for the parent to communicate her expectation and preannounce the consequences when those expectations aren't met. In other words, have a plan. Marriage and family therapist Dr. William Richardson says, "Without a plan, frustration and anger boil over. On the other hand, when we know what we will do next in a difficult situation, we experience more calm and control."[9]

The plan starts with the parent announcing the expectations for behavior. In my example above, let's pick one behavior, such as cleaning up dishes. I'm sure most parents have asked children to do this simple task many times. However, this time the mother is going to preannounce a logical consequence, one connected to the behavior. She might say something like this, "Leaving dirty dishes in the sink isn't how we care for our home. Please rinse your dishes and put them in the dishwasher. If you choose not to do this, I'll assume you need more practice. If I find dirty dishes in the sink again, you'll get practice by washing everyone's dishes after dinner for three days."

In this scenario the child knows the expectations and knows the consequences should he choose to ignore his mother's request. Dr. Richardson calls this "The Formula." The Formula works when "parents plan and announce:

- specific behaviors to be stopped
- specific behaviors to be started
- specific consequences to be used"[10]

In the first example, when I walked into the house to discover a mess, there was a clash of wills between the children and me. By following Dr. Richardson's Formula, the child isn't clashing with his mother and doesn't take it personally. He's clashing with the rules and fully aware that it's his choice. Mom doesn't take it personally either, and thereby her anger is reduced as well.

Finding logical consequences for each challenge in your home may take some time. I've discovered that the insight of friends can help when I'm stuck. We've even written consequences down. It takes extra effort up front, but it's worth it. This approach has worked amazingly well in our home and reduced many angry struggles between children, parents, and siblings.

Evaluate Your Own Heart

Sometimes the source of our children's anger lies within ourselves. In Matthew 7:3, we read the words of Jesus when He said, "Why do you look at the speck of sawdust in your brother's eye and pay no attention to the plank in your own eye?"

As we consider the pain that anger causes our children, it's important to consider how we use anger and how we can stir up anger in others—especially our children.

If you had asked me what my strongest character virtue was years ago, I might have said patience. Then I had children. My strong will collided with the daily sacrifice it takes to be a patient mother. Motherhood caused me to come face to face with many selfish desires that hadn't been uncovered before. Motherhood tested me and left me wanting.

Before addressing the anger in my children's hearts, I've had to address my own. God gently revealed a heart that sought its own way and comfort above sacrifice. It's a daily submission of my will to God's will. And honestly it's a battle some days. But it's one worth fighting. For through this submission process, God has changed me in good and humbling ways.

I can no longer say that patience is my strongest virtue. What I can boast about is God's grace and power in spite of my weakness. "But he said to me, 'My grace is sufficient for you, for my power is made perfect in weakness.' Therefore I will boast all the more gladly about my weaknesses, so that Christ's power may rest on me" (2 Corinthians 12:9).

Memory Verses

My dear brothers, take note of this: Everyone should be quick to listen, slow to speak and slow to become angry, for man's anger does not bring about the righteous life that God desires.

JAMES 1:19-20

In your anger do not sin: Do not let the sun go down while you are still angry, and do not give the devil a foothold.

EPHESIANS 4:26-27

But he said to me, "My grace is sufficient for you, for my power is made perfect in weakness." Therefore I will boast all the more gladly about my weaknesses, so that Christ's power may rest on me.

2 CORINTHIANS 12:9

Do not be quickly provoked in your spirit, for anger resides in the lap of fools.

ECCLESIASTES 7:9

A gentle answer turns away wrath, but
a harsh word stirs up anger.

PROVERBS 15:1

Encouraging Words

Speak when you are angry—and you'll
make the best speech you'll ever regret.

—DR. LAWRENCE J. PETER

The world needs anger. The world often continues
to allow evil because it isn't angry enough.

—BEDE JARRETT

Anger, if not restrained, is frequently more
hurtful to us than the injury that provokes it.

—SENECA

People who fly into a rage always make a bad landing.

—WILL ROGERS

The intoxication of anger, like that of the grape,
shows us to others, but hides us from ourselves.

—JOHN DRYDEN

Discussion or Journal Questions

1. Do you find it hard to think of any anger as good? If so, why?

2. Have you ever seen assertive anger used to bring about good? Give an example.

3. Is there injustice or wrongdoing in this world that deserves to have more people good and angry? What are some of those wrongs many of us tolerate?

4. Do your children exhibit any ongoing disobedient behaviors that should be addressed in order to reduce angry confrontations? List a few and identify logical consequences you can preannounce.

5. How has anger damaged you or someone you love?

6. Why is it easy to express anger and frustration to those we love?

7. What are some ways to deal with anger that don't hurt someone else?

8. Do you find your patience wearing thin at a specific time of day or regarding specific events? Evaluate changes you might need to make in order to ease your frustrations.

9. Write down some characteristics of a gentle and kind parent.

10. What is one commitment you can make to reduce harmful anger in your life?

Chapter Eleven

Investing in Your Child's Strengths

Little Boy Blue come blow your horn…

My son Dylan is a naturally athletic boy. From an early age, he excelled in team sports and showed a unique combination of confidence, aggressive but fair play, and leadership skills. Whether it was a YMCA team or other community organization, Dylan quickly rose to the top. His coaches appointed him team captain, and his teammates looked to him for direction. That was a strong combination of skills in elementary school, but things started to change in junior high.

One by one Dylan's friends started to grow, inching above and beyond 12-year-old Dylan's five-foot-one-inch stature. Voices lowered, hair sprouted, and muscles popped, while Dylan remained much the same. Junior high boys turned into men in a matter of months, while others kept their boyish looks. Still athletically gifted, the bar was raised as the competition level increased for Dylan. Height mattered. Strength dominated. While he excelled in long-distance running, Dylan just didn't have the short distance speed to compensate for his delayed growth.

This athletic and confident boy was devastated when he didn't make the school basketball team in seventh grade. He didn't make the football team either that year. We were all shocked because he particularly excelled in that sport. Up until that point, Dylan had been playing on teams assembled by age and weight, which leveled the playing field.

Seventh grade was a challenging year for all of us. School coaches frustrated us when they didn't see the same potential we saw. As parents my husband and I struggled to keep our negative thoughts to ourselves. Both of us entered puberty late. Dylan's older brother hadn't started "the change" until he was 14 and was dealing with the same issues in high school. We knew Dylan would grow, especially since my husband is six foot three and I'm five foot eight. But that promise didn't help Dylan as a sad seventh grader.

Realizing there was nothing we could do about his height, we determined to find other ways to encourage Dylan's love for sports and abilities to lead, and help him develop his natural talent. It just wasn't going to be on school teams. Thankfully he had already signed up for the community football team he'd been on for years and was able to have a very successful year helping his team advance to the state playoffs.

That was two years ago, and at the writing of this chapter, my son is a sophomore in high school. He's grown a few inches, and the testosterone is just now kicking in. Yes, the Whitwer family blooms late. Our oldest son finally experienced his growth spurt and now stands taller than his father. So there is hope.

Dylan's not alone in his frustration. Every day a child faces a limitation based on physical design or developmental stage. Many kids long to play a specific sport but discover they aren't fast enough, strong enough, or aggressive enough. Other kids want to perform, but someone can hit a higher note, dance a little better, or has a more dramatic personality. Children want to rank in the top of their class, but someone grasps chemistry or languages better than they do. Anger, tears, and blame can result from these frustrations. Unfortunately many kids grow up believing they are never good enough.

The Heartbreak of Not Being Good Enough

It is true someone will always be better, stronger, and faster than us. Unless a child has the natural ability to rationalize the situation, it's easy to see why kids give up and never reach their full potential.

After all a child often thinks, *Why even bother if I can't make the starting lineup?*

I bet every parent reading this book can easily return to their growing-up years and identify a similar situation. Mine was athletics. From an early age, the only sport I excelled in was tetherball. Some might argue that it is not a sport, but it was all I had. Honestly the only reason I could even play that sport was because of my height. By the time I got to fifth grade and a new playground without a tetherball, I realized my worst fear—there was nothing for me to do during recess. It didn't matter what sport it was. While playing volleyball, I bumped the ball backwards. During a softball game, I got hit in the head while trying to catch the ball. On the track I came in last. In speed-a-way I did all of the above. The list went on. My uncoordinated, slow body kept me on the sidelines.

I know the pain of being the last one picked for every team in PE. I had no expertise within myself to change the circumstances. My parents weren't active, so they couldn't help either. Unfortunately, by the beginning of junior high, I labeled myself as completely unathletic. I only tried out for a sport one more time. It was in high school, at the begging of a friend who wanted me to try out with her. I didn't make the team, and after that, I gave up trying. Inactivity became my way of life.

The good news for your children and me is God has given us many strengths. An early introduction to music saved my heart from a self-esteem meltdown over my lack of sports acumen. For whatever reason, the grade school I attended offered chorus as an option for third graders. That seems crazy to me now, but it was a dream come true. As an eight-year-old, I learned I could hold a note and that I liked singing harmony. Even though I didn't have any natural athletic ability, I could sing!

My mother realized it too. She saw my love for music, and from that point on, she was my biggest supporter. Her love and unconditional support of how God made me—not athletic, but musical—fed my need for affirmation and acceptance of how God made me. She sewed my choral costumes and never missed a concert. As I got into high school and joined a Christian band, it didn't matter if our concerts were in the back of a pizza place or at a large church, she was always in the audience. She'd heard the same songs a hundred times, but she was there.

My mother saw a seed of natural ability and invested in that talent. She valued the ability I had and encouraged me to pursue my best in singing. Although my lack of athletic ability frustrated me, the support I got at home for my true strengths was like a rock solid foundation in the shifting sands of elementary school.

Allow Your Child to Grieve if Necessary

Coming to grips with our personal limitations is painful at any age. As adults we have the advantage of watching God bring good out of our past challenges. We know that if God closes one door, He is already planning to open another. But a child only sees a door slammed in her face. Trying to hurry past a child's pain can seem insensitive to her.

Sarah Peppel vividly remembers her mother's actions at the darkest time in her high school years:

> The end of tenth grade was tough for me when in one week I learned that I had been out-cheered for the cheerleading squad, out-voted for student government, and out-dramatized for the school play. I cried for a whole day. I look back on how my mom helped me overcome that fateful Saturday that changed the course of high school and my life, and the first thing I remember is my mom letting me have my day of grief. She comforted me and then left me alone to cry it out and realize for myself that life was not going to end.
>
> I am sure that at some point we prayed. My mother was a strong Christian and had ingrained in us over the years the overwhelming sense that God is in control and that everything would be okay, given time. I don't think I was listening closely that day, but I am sure it was there in her hugs and

tissues for my tears. I was reflecting more on the "valley of the shadow of death" in Psalm 23, to be morbidly precise.

Sarah's mother continued to help her daughter recover, and I'll tell you the rest of the story in a few paragraphs.

Identify the Core Strengths

One of the gifts we can give our children is to identify their natural core strengths. We all have them. The problem with most of us is twofold when trying to identify strengths: (1) We look at the end result, and (2) we look for obvious strengths.

For example, if we are looking to identify a strength in Josh, we might look for success at the *end* of his efforts. We might look at his grades or if he made the school team. We could consider his record in a given sport or if he made first chair in the band. Basically we look to see if the end result was successful according to a common societal definition of success. If his grades aren't stellar, then we might mentally label him weak in all areas of academia.

The second common misconception is to look for the popular and most obvious strengths. In children, athletic ability is probably considered first, followed by social and then academic success. We value these three visible strengths in society, and children who don't meet the strict criteria for success can easily become discouraged, thinking they have no talent.

But hidden underneath the obvious are core strengths that are even more valuable for a parent to identify. If we can identify these hidden strengths, we can help our children develop into the young men and women God means for them to be. Hidden strengths often last over the years, and God commonly uses them to fulfill His work here on earth.

Consider Moses. At face value Moses didn't have much obvious personal strength. He could have been ruling over Egypt, alongside his adopted family, but after murdering a man, he goes into hiding in the desert and cares for sheep. Moses didn't have the obvious gifts of leadership, charisma, or physical strength that we know. But God knew Moses had talent hidden under those weaknesses. God saw an obedient, loyal, and teachable servant. God nurtured those strengths, and Moses developed into a mighty leader. Moses wasn't perfect in those areas, but God used him.

When parents identify core strengths in children, they can help reroute their children when they hit a dead end. An example would be the child who is highly curious about a given subject, but this natural interest doesn't translate into a high grade. This child could just be a poor test taker at this point in her life. Parents should encourage this curiosity. Depending on the subject matter, a child could get involved in junior programs sponsored by museums, universities, national or state parks, hobbyists, or even the military. There are probably more opportunities to develop that core strength than you initially think.

This skill of identifying a core strength can be helpful for children who excel in the most obvious of the skill areas. Even naturally athletic children can face limitations based on the sports that are available to them and who is making the coaching decisions. If the child has a core competitive nature simmering below the natural athletic talent, they can develop this strength off the playing field in a different setting, such as the debate club or in an academic competition.

Find Another Outlet

After allowing Sarah time to grieve, her mother helped her recover by gently redirecting her daughter to other interests. Sarah remembers, "Not wanting me to hurt, she turned my attention to short-term, lovely matters that would cheer my soul and give me more time to rest my heart while my mind sorted out the details." But her mother didn't stop there. She offered unconditional support for Sarah to try out again for cheerleading, student government, or the play. She encouraged Sarah to try new things as well.

Together they explored Sarah's creative side with pottery classes. Her mother identified her core strength of caring for others and introduced community service, which became a growing passion for Sarah.

Through her parents' support at the darkest time of her teenage years, Sarah discovered one of her callings in life. "My budding interest in community service changed the focus and direction of my life and has served ever since as a means of glorifying the Lord in my daily walk with Him."

In our family we have continued to support Dylan and discovered a sport he excels in—wrestling. This sport is an ideal outlet for our competitive son. Dylan only wrestles boys within a few pounds of his weight, and he only measures his success against his own performances. Additionally his wrestling coach is a strong Christian man, forging the mission field of a public high school and teaching character building along with the sport. It's been a fantastic experience for all of us.

Through this experience we've felt the heartache that comes when a child longs to do something, but his body isn't in sync with his desires. We've focused on our son's natural strengths and invested time, energy, and finances into those areas. We've accepted the reality that there are weaknesses we can't change. Above all we have had to trust that God knew exactly what He was doing when He designed Dylan.

Compare Yourself to Yourself

We have all grown up in a culture when at a very early age, we learn to rate ourselves based on others. Especially girls. However, both boys and girls learn to base their value on how they compare to those around them. Most self-aware kids can rank themselves in any given group within minutes. They know where they rate in popularity, intelligence, and ability.

Once that ranking happens and a child identifies himself on the low end of the totem pole, it doesn't seem to matter what his seed of natural talent is. If they compare themselves to someone who seems to have more talent, many children quickly give up on themselves. They might even subconsciously assume a "why bother?" mentality and apathy can easily set in.

The solution according to Sean Flannigan, high school coach and teacher of gifted classes, is to teach kids at an early age to compare themselves with themselves. Flannigan observes this challenge every day as a coach and teacher:

> The driving thing I do as a coach is to get kids to have the mentality that you can have success or failure based on what you do and how you push yourself. When I was coaching track, I saw this the most. Out of all the sports, we find that in track pure, natural athletic ability is more important than anything. There was a kid who was blazing fast, but he would party all night. He'd show up in the morning hung over and sleep under a tree until it was his turn to run, then he'd win. Kids could work as hard as they wanted, but if they didn't have the quick reflexes and the right muscle tissue, they just couldn't do it. So I started trying to teach them to compare yourself to yourself. When you first came in, you could run an eight-minute mile. Now you are down to a six-thirty. Yeah, even though that kid can run a five-fifteen mile, he doesn't work as hard as you. He should be running a sub-five mile.

As parents, we can help our children develop this practice by keeping track of milestones in their development. My kids marvel at the pantry wall with black lines and dates marking their growth through the years. They love to see how much they have grown in the past year or five years. To help your children develop the practice of monitoring progress in terms of their own growth in a specific area, consider starting a journal and recording significant stages of development. For example if a child starts playing the violin at age eight and begins with book one, keep track of when they move from book to book. This will be a source of encouragement if they grow discouraged or plateau in their progress.

Don't Give Up Too Soon

As caring parents we all want to see our children succeed in something they love. What happens when our child loves something but doesn't have any apparent natural talent in that area? One of the most dangerous things a parent can do is give up too soon.

Just because your child doesn't show the talent of a prodigy, he could still develop talent and ability over time. Flannigan observes a phenomenon that often happens when athletes enter high school after being a superstar in grade school: "Some kids just tear it up in junior high, but by their junior year in high school, they are riding the bench. A lot has to do with development. Some people physically mature earlier than others."

This same thing can happen with any natural ability. If a child doesn't pair ability with good work habits, she can burn out over time. As parents we can help our children develop discipline until their physical, emotional, or mental abilities develop to their fullest capacity.

We all need some of the same foundational skills to be successful in any endeavor. We can help prepare our children for future success by focusing on the disciplines of practice, perseverance, working with others, respect for authority, giving our best, and honoring God by using the abilities He has given.

When Should a Child Quit?

One question most parents struggle with is when to allow a child to quit something. Whether it's piano lessons, a sports team, or student council, many children will become discouraged and want to quit. What's a parent to do—force them to stick it out or allow them to move on?

In Scripture God consistently values those with a steadfast heart. We are told to stand firm in the face of fear and an enemy (2 Chronicles 20:17), stand up against temptation (1 Corinthians 10:13), and to take a stand against the devil's schemes (Ephesians 6:10-18). We see God's character revealed in His persistent love and faithfulness, in spite of our lack of both. Staying committed, in spite of trials, is a godly virtue that is worth sewing into our children's lives.

However, there does come a time when it's in our children's best interest to back out of a commitment. Those times might include when there is ongoing sinful behavior on the part of those in leadership, abuse of any kind, or danger due to neglect. Of course, if a child's health declines due to serious illness, that's an obvious reason to quit.

Depending on the age of the child, it also might be appropriate to withdraw from a commitment if there are significant behavioral changes that you can't trace to a specific incident. Children aren't always able to tell us when something inappropriate is happening. Behavioral changes are often a clue that something needs our attention.

Poor reasons for quitting include an "unfair" coach, a teacher who plays favorites, "mean" teammates, or a child who is just tired of the activity. Those are the times to focus on other life skills, such as dealing with difficult people and finishing the commitment with integrity. We can teach our children to guard their tongues instead of complain, to work hard even though their potential is overlooked, and finish well.

God Doesn't See Things the Same Way

In America we focus on obvious strengths: leadership, athletics, academics, external beauty, and artistic talent. We easily identify these strengths, and parents, teachers, coaches, and society in general applaud and encourage them. All of these talents and natural gifts are good, especially when we acknowledge God gave them and intended them for use in building up His church.

Unfortunately many children and parents focus on those external strengths and desire them above all others. But God has another litmus test for strengths—those that are hidden.

We learn this lesson in the book of 1 Samuel, after God rejected Saul as king of Israel. Saul was a powerful and effective king. He amassed an army of 200,000 foot soldiers plus 10,000 more from the tribe of Judah. Then, upon the command of the Lord, Saul led his men and attacked the Amalekites. God gave Saul and his army the victory and told him to destroy *all* living things. Saul, however, decided to spare the best of the sheep and cattle.

We might justify this slight deviation from God's command just as Saul did. After all we could rationalize that these strong animals could be used for many things, including offering them back as a sacrifice to God. But God didn't agree with Saul's thinking. In fact God was "grieved" that Saul disobeyed Him and that He had made Saul king. God then asked Samuel, God's prophet, to give Saul the bad news that he was no longer king.

Samuel's immediate assignment following the deposition of Saul as king was to find the next king. God directed Samuel to the town of Bethlehem and told him to initiate a sacrifice and invite a man named Jesse and his sons to attend. God had already chosen one of those sons as the next king. Samuel obeyed God and waited and watched with interest as Jesse arrived with seven of his sons.

First Samuel 16:6-7 tells the story of what happened next. "When they arrived, Samuel saw Eliab and thought, 'Surely the LORD's anointed stands here before the LORD.' But the LORD said to Samuel, 'Do not consider his appearance or his height, for I have rejected him. The LORD does not look at the things man looks at. Man looks at the outward appearance, but the LORD looks at the heart.'"

One by one Jesse's sons passed in front of Samuel. One by one God rejected them. Samuel must have been confused because God told him one of these boys would be king. The sons Samuel had seen were strong young men. Could there have been a mistake? Samuel, confident of God's command, asked the father if there were any other sons. Yes, came the answer. The youngest one was tending the sheep.

Scripture doesn't say, but Jesse must have been told that Samuel was looking for a king before coming to the sacrifice. Jesse must have brought the sons who seemed destined for greatness. Too unimportant to come to the sacrifice, too small to be a possibility, little David was left at home. His earthly father overlooked his potential for greatness—but not his heavenly Father.

When David appeared before Samuel, God confirmed His choice. "Then the LORD said, 'Rise and anoint him; he is the one'" (1 Samuel 16:12).

God looked beyond what the world saw, which was a young boy with no apparent strengths, no physical ability to set him apart, no wisdom visible at an early age, and no talent beyond herding some dirty sheep. Just a boy. God saw something more valuable than obvious strengths.

God saw a heart of passion for the things of the Lord, bravery waiting to be tested, and humility hidden deep. God saw a servant king, one who would foreshadow the coming Messiah. Although David was a flawed man, God knew his true strengths were within.

Identifying a God-Given Strength

Consider God as a master painter. Rick Warren says, "You are God's handcrafted work of art. You are not an assembly-line product, mass produced without thought. You are a custom-designed, one-of-a-kind original masterpiece."[1] In His plan to create you and your child, He colored your life with certain characteristics such as:

- Personality
- Likes and dislikes
- Talents
- Physical ability
- Learning style
- Spiritual gifting

The fact that your child would rather read a book than play football isn't a mistake. It's a God-given design, and God has a plan to use that love of words.

The Bible tells us that God also gives spiritual gifts to those who believe in Him (1 Corinthians 12). If your child has accepted Jesus as his or her Savior, then God has already given your child one or more gifts. God asks us to use these gifts to serve Him through His church. When we understand our gifts and use them with the right motives, God blesses and grows them. You can give your children a boost in this area by helping them identify these gifts early. I have discovered the greatest joys in my life come when I am serving God according to my gifts. Otherwise I'm just stressed out from trying to work outside my natural gifting.

To get an idea of some of the spiritual gifts, read the following Scriptures:

- 1 Corinthians 12
- Romans 12
- Ephesians 4

Most churches offer a spiritual gifts test to help you identify your gifts. If you would like to pursue this more, please speak with one of your pastors.

The Returns Are Great on This Investment

We can't count on stock market gains, but we can count on an investment in our child's strengths. Not only do the returns guarantee a greater enjoyment of life for our child, but we are helping to prepare them for serving God. When we look at their lives with a big-picture view, we can identify strengths that others miss. It's a win-win situation for everyone.

Memory Verses

For we are God's workmanship, created in Christ Jesus to do good works, which God prepared in advance for us to do.

EPHESIANS 2:10

But now, this is what the LORD says—he who created you, O Jacob, he who formed you, O Israel: "Fear not, for I have redeemed you; I have summoned you by name; you are mine."

ISAIAH 43:21

Your hands shaped me and made me.

JOB 10:8

*Each one should use whatever gift he has
received to serve others, faithfully administering
God's grace in its various forms.*

1 PETER 4:10

*Whatever you do, work at it with all your heart,
as working for the Lord, not for men.*

COLOSSIANS 3:23

Encouraging Words

*What you are is God's gift to you; what you
do with yourself is your gift to God.*

—DANISH PROVERB

*Everyone who got where he is has
had to begin where he was.*

—ROBERT LOUIS STEVENSON

We will either find a way, or make one.

—HANNIBAL

*Do not pray for easy lives. Pray to be stronger
men! Do not pray for tasks equal to your
powers. Pray for power equal to your tasks.*

—PHILLIPS BROOKS

*Hide not your talents, they for use were
made. What's a sundial in the shade?*

—BENJAMIN FRANKLIN

We are not retreating—we are
advancing in another direction.
—Douglas MacArthur

Discussion or Journal Questions

1. What are some of the weaknesses you have struggled with over the years?

2. Can you look back on your life and see early signs of natural talents that might have been overlooked by others?

3. Why do we often want talents and strengths that others have?

4. Why is it dangerous to compare ourselves and our natural or spiritual gifts to others?

5. What hinders parents from identifying and accepting their child's natural abilities?

6. What are some of your child's passions?

7. What holds us back from pursuing our God-given strengths?

8. If we understand that spiritual gifts are given to benefit the church as a whole (1 Corinthians 12:7), why is it so important to help our children identify theirs?

9. List five of your child's core strengths.

10. What are some ways you can encourage your child's natural abilities?

Chapter Twelve

Overcoming Insecurity

Wednesday's child is full of woe...

Our daughter Cathrine joined the Whitwer family in the fall of 2005. She didn't join our family in the traditional way, which would be after nine months of pregnancy and ten hours of labor. Cathrine journeyed a different path. Her story started in war-torn Liberia, Africa in 1995. Her first ten years involved desperate survival—never enough food, no education, and little compassion. When I watched her walk down the airport walkway holding my husband's hand, her little face was bleak and scared. She barely raised her eyes to see her new family.

Her younger sister, Ruth, on the other hand, was immediately part of the family. She wanted someone to hold her, enjoyed the spotlight, and lavished affection on us all. Cathrine was a different story. Although they shared the same birth mother, we've learned she treated the girls differently. Their mother adored Ruth and blamed Cathrine for everything her impetuous little sister did.

As a result our oldest daughter was a picture of insecurity. It was obvious nothing she did was ever good enough. Thankfully God gave us great compassion for her mother. We know she did the best she could in very hopeless circumstances, so we place no blame. However, we had a challenge to invest confidence in this beautiful child, who is now our daughter.

The goal of this book is to help parents deal with the everyday hurts of life. I resisted telling Cathrine's story because it's not an everyday story. Her background and her early childhood deprivation are quite unique. Also she doesn't look like the other children, even those who share her dark coloring. She doesn't speak like the other children, and she doesn't process information through the grid of American thought. However, I see the same need for confidence that I see in my other children. In the three years she has been part of our family, we have seen a remarkable transformation.

Cathrine no longer walks with her head down, nor does she cling to our hands and cry in a new situation. Although she struggles significantly with education, she approaches it with confidence. She attends church camp and makes friends. She tries scary rides at the theme parks and proudly buys the pin to prove she did it. She's a strong contributing member to her soccer team. Cathrine is absolute proof that parents can help an insecure child, even with painful experiences in her background.

Cathrine's struggle with insecurity is not unlike what many children in America face, only for different reasons. Dr. James Dobson wrote, "The current epidemic of self-doubt has resulted from a totally unjust and unnecessary system of evaluating human worth. This system is prevalent in our society. Not everyone is deemed worthy; not everyone is accepted. Instead, we reserve our praise and admiration for a select few who have been blessed from birth with the characteristics we value most highly."[1]

It is the rare child who does not compare herself to others and find herself wanting in some area—either beauty, intelligence, creativity, or athletics. In this superficial world, is it possible to develop a deep self-confidence that's unrelated to our exterior accomplishments? Absolutely! It starts with understanding that we can find our value in who we are as children of God. Then we add to that a commitment on our part to think, speak, and act counterculture to the message that bombards our children's minds every day—the one that implies that they can embrace their value based on how they look and perform.

Why Some Kids Suffer More than Others

Our son Dylan entered this world with a confident grin and a bold step. Even at the age of two, we noticed something different about him. He would look an adult in the eye, thrust out his little hand for a firm shake, and address them by his or her first and last name. Dylan's confidence paved the way for a smooth grade school experience and is easing his time in high school.

Although Dylan grew up in the same environment as his brothers, they don't have the same level of confidence. They are more hesitant to join a group of boys playing basketball and would rather try something new with a friend by their side than alone. They aren't as confident in their success as Dylan.

As I've pondered this difference in my children, I realized their upbringing wasn't exactly the same. Dylan's brothers had some challenges early on. Joshua wore glasses at the age of 11 months, which affected much of his balance and depth of vision and was detrimental to a young boy trying to learn sports. Robbie didn't wear glasses but had a severe speech problem. This influenced Robbie's confidence in reading out loud, meeting new people, and introducing himself.

While they are growing in their confidence, it isn't at the same level their brother experiences. I've realized a truth about confidence. A child's confidence doesn't erode in a week, nor is it restored quickly. When a child struggles with insecurity, it takes consistency and patience to build their confidence. Do not despair if you don't see immediate results. Perseverance will bring about a harvest of confidence.

You Belong!

A few years ago I spoke at a parenting conference on the subject of "Raising Faithful Kids in a Faithless World." As research for the talk, I asked young adults with a strong Christian faith what their parents did right. I put together a survey, and with our youth director's help, handed it out to young adults between the ages of 17 and 25. These are what I call the "dark ages," when many kids turn away from the faith they embraced as a child. I wanted to know why these young adults remained faithful.

I asked them two questions:

1. What *general* things did your parents do right to help your faith grow and mature?

2. What *specific* things did they do that helped strengthen your faith as a child and teenager?

I summarized their responses and came up with eight practices parents can implement to help their child's faith become real as they grow up. The number one response surprised me. It was to have family standards.

Family standards, traditions, and rituals are extraordinarily important to kids. That's true in my house. If we have pizza two Friday nights in a row, we have started a family tradition that better not be broken. More important than fun shared experiences, family standards communicate to a child that she belongs in the family and is part of a team. Children grow up thinking, *We believe this and we act in this way*, and it develops a connection between parents and children.

Dr. Kevin Leman, in his book *Bringing Up Kids Without Tearing Them Down*, makes this observation: "When a child feels he belongs, he tells himself, 'I am worth something. I'm important. I fit in.' Children don't get very far in life before they run smack into situations where they're 'on the outside looking in.' They aren't welcome in the 'in group.'"[2]

Family unity may not seem like an obvious source of self-confidence, but to our children it means a lot. Every investment you make in your family is also an investment in each child's confidence level.

Start a Family Tradition

No matter the ages of your children, it's never too late to start a family tradition. As you consider this idea for your family, keep in mind that traditions don't have to be expensive. Some of the best traditions are simple, easy to maintain, and are opportunities to affirm the best in your children.

Growing up, we had one simple, yet memorable bedtime routine, which turned into a tradition. I don't remember a night when, after my mother tucked me in, I didn't get the same good night message: "Good night, my beautiful, sweet, wonderful, lovely daughter." To which I would reply: "Good night, my beautiful, sweet, wonderful, lovely mother." It was almost like a blessing my mother spoke over me each night, affirming my value to her. Unfortunately I wasn't always a sweet daughter, having a pretty sassy mouth at times. But my mother's words affirmed the best in me.

An easy way to start a tradition is with a holiday. Red breakfast is a big deal on Valentine's Day at my friend Ginny's house. Three of her kids are adults now, but everyone makes their way back home for red pancakes, strawberries, red fruit juice, and more.

Consider making spiritual traditions as well. At the Whitwer house, we pray with every child almost every night. As my oldest son turns 17, it is amazing to hear him say, "Mom, will you pray for me?"

My friend Cheri tells how her mother assigned her and her brother a Bible passage to read every morning. At breakfast the three of them discussed the reading for the day. Through that ritual, Cheri learned God's Word and connected with her mother and brother. Simple practices can make big spiritual impacts.

Write a Family Creed

Creed comes from the Latin "I believe." I grew up reciting the Apostles Creed in church, and it gave me a sense of pride, to be standing among men and women I had respected for years, reciting words that were really more than words—they were the foundation upon which I built my faith and life.

A creed shouldn't be limited to stating our historical Christian beliefs. Many families have discovered great benefits from creating their own family creed. A family creed should be created with every member of the family having input and state the core beliefs your family holds. Here are some possible components of a family creed:

- What we believe
- Character values that are important to us
- How we want to treat each other
- What we do together
- What our responsibilities as a family are

This document can change as you identify other important components or as your needs change. Make sure it's a document you don't hide in a drawer or scrapbook but is something you see everyday.

Not only does a creed unite your family, but it can also be used to establish truth in a world where truth is relevant and kids are swayed to and fro by the shifting winds of differing opinions.

Teach God's Truth as a Firm Foundation

In our postmodern world, many children, including those within the church, have a distorted view of God's truth. In essence they are building their house on sand instead of a rock. We know what happens to a house built on sand when the tide rises. Not only will their lives fall apart, but they will blame God when it does.

Postmodern thought claims truth does not exist in an objective sense. In other words, no truth exists outside of one's personal beliefs. Postmodern thinking also allows for specific cultures or communities of people to create their own truth. Basically it says, "What's true for me, isn't true for you."

I had the privilege of hearing Josh McDowell speak a few years ago regarding his book *Beyond Belief,* in which he addresses this issue of postmodern thought and its negative impact on our children. He told us about the time when he asked the same two questions to group after group of Christian kids and received the same two answers each time. McDowell asked, "Is the Bible true?" "Yes" was the consistent answer. He then asked, "How do you know it's true?" He was shocked when one after another answered, "Because I believe it."

Do you see the difference? It's not true because it came from God.

It's true to young people because they choose to believe it's true. This way of thinking not only erodes the foundation of faith, but it slowly and deceptively destroys a child's self-confidence. If they can't believe what God says is true, then what can they believe?

As parents we can counteract this wrong thinking by teaching the Bible as truth because God authored it. I've already mentioned the importance of believing what God says about us is true, but there are other biblical truths that profoundly impact our sense of self-worth and personal confidence. Here are some that have helped form my foundational sense of worth:

- God is always for me (Romans 8:28).
- God cares about the little details of my life (Luke 12:6-7).
- God does not treat me with anger (Psalm 86:15).
- God will be my defender (Psalm 12).
- God gives me wisdom (James 1:5).

God gave us the Bible as a gift to be used for many reasons. It has the power to transform lives through its authoritative truths. If your child struggles with insecurity, there is nothing like the Word of God to establish a firm foundation. "Every word of God is flawless; he is a shield to those who take refuge in him" (Proverbs 30:5).

The Problem with People Pleasing

People pleasing wreaks havoc on your confidence. What pleases one person displeases another. It's a constant losing game because you can't please everyone. Your subconscious knows this to be true, and you end up feeling like a failure most of the time.

Dr. Timothy Jennings, in his book *Could It Be This Simple?*, tells of Ethel, a pastor's wife who struggled with low self-esteem due to her people-pleasing tendencies. When Ethel was a young wife and student, the church organist called and asked her to fill in for her at midweek worship. Ethel really needed to study that night for a test but didn't know how to say no. She didn't want the organist to be mad at her, so Ethel cancelled her study plans and played. After this incident, Ethel's self-esteem, self-confidence, and self-worth all fell, not because playing the organ was bad but because of how Ethel made the decision. Dr. Jennings writes:

> Her self-esteem plummeted because she made a decision based on feelings of fear and insecurity, not on truth and facts. She went against her own judgment and allowed emotions of fear and insecurity to control her. In her own mind she experienced herself as weak and vacillating. As a consequence, she lost respect for herself.[3]

Ethel needed to make her decision based on her priorities and convictions, not emotions. Given the exact same circumstance, playing the organ that night could have been the right decision for someone else. But because Ethel did it out of fear or guilt, it was the wrong decision for her.

Our children face similar situations all the time. They want to please a teacher, fit in with a certain group, or make us happy. What parent hasn't used the people-pleasing tool to get a child to do some task around the house? "It will make Mommy very happy if you clean your room!" or "If you really loved me, you would do better at school."

Perhaps through our own words and behaviors, we unwittingly create children who look to others for approval and then find themselves insecure when it's not readily given. This might involve a gut check to see if we are using controlling or guilt-producing words. While it is good to make sacrifices for others, we should teach our children to do so out of love, not guilt.

See Your Child's Potential

One thing I love about God is that He believes in me. Even when I fall, even when I make a parenting mistake, even when I want to quit, He still believes in me. He still sees the potential in me. And He sees your potential too.

A few years ago, one of my children (who shall remain nameless) made a very bad choice. It devastated me because I never saw it coming, and it was so out of character for this child. I wrestled with my thoughts because honestly they were tending toward despair. Based on this one mistake, my scared and desperate mind had created a scenario where this child was on the path to a life without God and a life of sin.

That seems ridiculous now, but at the time, I was so afraid, and I wasn't thinking straight. I regret some of the accusatory and negative words I spoke. Very quickly God took me aside, and I got a talking-to. God reminded me of a few things. First, the good that was in my child was still there. Second, that child's sins were no different than mine. Third, God wasn't giving up on that child, and neither should I. I'm so glad God set me straight because I recovered from that incident and my child did too.

When we look past our children's outward behavior, their childish mistakes, and their bad choices and see their potential, we are giving them a dose of God-sized confidence. The world will give up on them, their teachers might give up on them, their friends may grow tired of them, but knowing their parent believes in them is priceless. More importantly God will never give up on them.

Help Your Child Get Back Up

Peter wanted to quit. Boy, did he ever. He had failed big time. What made it bad was he actually boasted that he wouldn't fail. But even worse, his failure involved betraying his best friend.

On the night the authorities arrested Jesus, Peter denied knowing Him three times. How could this happen? Was everything Peter previously claimed a lie? Did Peter really love Jesus? Was Peter really committed to following Jesus?

I'm sure Peter's thoughts ran along similar lines. This betrayal must have shaken Peter's confidence to the core. The Bible tells us that after he denied knowing Jesus a third time, Peter "went outside and wept bitterly" (Matthew 26:75).

After the crucifixion the disciples were devastated. I'm sure Peter had discounted himself and felt unworthy to be called a follower of Jesus. Even after the resurrection, Peter returned to what he knew before meeting Jesus, which was fishing.

One morning Peter set out in a boat to fish with some of the other disciples, but their nets remained empty. Suddenly a man yelled from the shore, telling them to try the other side of the boat. When they did, their nets were full, and immediately they recognized the man as Jesus. They made their way over to the shore, where Jesus had started a small fire and was cooking some fish.

Jesus had appeared to the disciples before, but this was Peter's first time to confront the friend and Savior he had betrayed. Although there was joy in seeing Jesus alive, I imagine Peter's heart pounded in his chest with fear. What would Jesus say?

The Bible records this amazing conversation in John 21:15-17:

> When they had finished eating, Jesus said to Simon Peter, "Simon son of John, do you truly love me more than these?"
>
> "Yes, Lord," he said, "you know that I love you."
>
> Jesus said, "Feed my lambs."
>
> Again Jesus said, "Simon son of John, do you truly love me?"
>
> He answered, "Yes, Lord, you know that I love you."
>
> Jesus said, "Take care of my sheep."
>
> The third time he said to him, "Simon son of John, do you love me?"
>
> Peter was hurt because Jesus asked him the third time, "Do you love me?" He said, "Lord, you know all things; you know that I love you."
>
> Jesus said, "Feed my sheep."

Jesus knew Peter's confidence was in shreds at that moment. Not only had Peter been devastated by his own behavior, but Peter also was unsure about what would happen to everything he had believed in and worked for during the past three years. Yes, Peter knew that Jesus had come back to life. But what did that mean for Peter's life?

At that moment Jesus looked into Peter's eyes and spoke the words that surely brought meaning and hope to Peter's life: *Feed my sheep.* In other words, I'm not done with you yet, Peter. I know you are weak right now, but I have plans for you. And I trust you with those plans. Feed my sheep.

We know from Scripture that Peter rose to the challenge. From that moment on, Peter's boldness and confidence were matched by his depth of character. He joined his small band of friends, and through the power of the Holy Spirit, changed the world with the gospel of Jesus Christ.

As parents we can give our children the same gift of boldness and confidence. When they fall—and they will fall—we have the opportunity to hold out a hand, help them get up, and invite them to try again. We can communicate the same life-changing message that Jesus gave to Peter: I know you feel weak, but God's got a plan for you. Get up. And each time we plant that seed of confidence, a little bit of insecurity melts away.

Memory Verses

You have been my hope, O Sovereign
LORD, my confidence since my youth.

PSALM 71:5

"For I know the plans I have for you," declares
the LORD, "plans to prosper you and not to harm
you, plans to give you a hope and a future."

JEREMIAH 29:11

He chose us in him before the creation of the
world to be holy and blameless in his sight.

EPHESIANS 1:4

Every word of God is flawless; he is a shield
to those who take refuge in him.

PROVERBS 30:5

The LORD will be your confidence and will
keep your foot from being snared.

PROVERBS 3:26

Encouraging Words

Insist on yourself; never imitate.

—RALPH WALDO EMERSON

Confidence is contagious. So is lack of confidence.

—VINCE LOMBARDI

It is not the mountain we conquer but ourselves.

—SIR EDMUND HILLARY

Where I found truth, there found I my
God, who is the truth itself.

—AUGUSTINE

Start with what is right rather than what is acceptable.

—FRANZ KAFKA

Aim at heaven and you will get earth thrown
in. Aim at earth and you get neither.

—C.S. LEWIS

Discussion or Journal Questions

1. List two or three God-given characteristics that you like about yourself.

2. Identify two ways you determine your opinion about yourself.

3. How might your life change if your self-confidence was defined only by what God thinks of you?

4. Proverbs 3:5 states, "Trust in the LORD with all your heart and lean not on your own understanding." How does depending on our own understanding undermine our confidence?

5. How does forming opinions of yourself and the world around you on God's truth develop confidence?

6. Has the desire to please other people ever led you or your child down a wrong path? Explain.

7. On the other hand, have you ever made a decision that wasn't popular, but it was based on God's truth? How did that turn out?

8. What undermines your child's confidence the most?

9. Do you ever find yourself holding back from offering God your best? What are some reasons for that?

10. In what areas of your life can you offer Jesus more?

Chapter Thirteen

Dealing with a Bully

Kissed the girls and made them cry...

It was the start of seventh grade, and my youngest son, Robbie, asked what seemed like an innocent question: "Mom, what would you and Dad do if I got into a fight?"

Initially I thought Robbie was simply being speculative. After all, I knew boys got into fights. Through the years I'd heard stories about who was meeting whom behind the school or at the park. Fights are a thing of joy to most young men. With a little enhancing and retelling, they turn into legendary epic battles. Robbie was probably just exploring the idea from all sides in case it ever happened, I reasoned.

But it did force me to ask the most important question: *Why wasn't Robbie asking his dad this?* Aren't moms supposed to help boys understand why a girl who likes him would hit him? I could answer that question...kind of. I just wasn't prepared to get into a discussion on the finer points of street fighting with my preteen.

Nevertheless, Robbie asked me, and I needed to respond. There wasn't a precedent because his two older brothers had never gotten into a fight—at least not that I knew of. They never brought home stories of bullies challenging them or stories of them initiating a brawl. We certainly had other social issues, but bullying and fighting didn't seem to be on our list of problems.

As I formulated my answer to Robbie's question, I forced myself to make a decision about what I really believed about solving problems in a physical way. Of course, I was against it. I'm a firm believer in solving problems in a peaceful way. But I got stuck in my mental processing when I pictured my son backed up against a wall by a bully, fear in his eyes, and no peaceful outcome in sight. What then?

My husband and I talked about it to make sure we were in agreement. Then, when I had my thoughts in a coherent manner, I sat down with Robbie. My answer was simple and went something like this: "Robbie, if you throw the first punch, you will be in trouble. That's not how we deal with our anger or solve problems. But you have our permission to defend yourself if need be. And you have our permission to defend someone weaker who is being attacked. If you are honestly defending yourself or someone else, you will not get in trouble at home."

He understood our stance and seemed satisfied. I breathed a sigh of relief, feeling proud of myself at having handled that so easily. In fact I was confident, concluding that Robbie's questions were only out of curiosity because this wasn't a problem in our home. Little did I know our bully-free days were about to change, and my attitude and convictions would be severely tested.

Two weeks later Robbie came home from school and announced that a boy who had picked on him for a while asked to meet him after school. The meeting was scheduled for the next day; time and place confirmed. My eyes widened, and I struggled with what to say. Should I tell him, "Absolutely not!"? Or should I allow him to show up? My attitude about bullies was all fine and good in theory, but now the reality of it was staring me in the face.

The worst part of it all? My husband was in Africa. I needed to handle this situation alone. I couldn't even call or e-mail my husband for advice. The first place to start seemed obvious—desperate prayers. So I prayed for wisdom above and beyond what I could muster in my own strength and from experience. My heart was telling me one thing, but my head was telling me another. Could I trust my heart, which was telling me to protect my son at all cost? Or should I trust my head, which was telling me I had to allow my son to defend his honor?

Every dangerous possibility went through my head. I've watched enough news programs to realize that kids can do very violent things to each other. But I also know that parents have sent their children to school or church, thinking they were safe there, only to find out they weren't. The reality is that we cannot fully protect our children anywhere—even at home—without God's divine intervention.

So I reviewed what I knew about bullies: (1) Don't let a bully know you are afraid; (2) always be with a buddy; and (3) stand up for yourself. I realize my decision will seem very controversial to some of you, but I let my son face the bully.

Robbie's rationale about showing up made sense to me and was in line with what I had read. Robbie wanted this boy to know he wasn't afraid of him and that it wasn't okay to be a bully. It was Robbie's plan to diffuse the situation by talking with this other boy and asking him to stop picking on him. I made sure he had an older friend with him— one who had a cell phone. We discussed all the possibilities and how to handle them, including what to do if this other boy tried anything physical. Then I allowed my son to do what he needed to do to defend his honor…while I waited around the corner and prayed.

Fifteen minutes later Robbie and his friend walked in the door singing "We Are the Champions," completely unscathed. Turns out the bully stayed home. More than 20 boys had gathered to watch what might happen, and they all saw that my son showed up while the bully didn't.

What a difference this response made to this other boy. Immediately the bullying stopped at school. Robbie even said they became friends.

Did we make the right decision? For this child, for this circumstance, and for this type of bullying, it would seem that we did. Was this the right response for every situation of bullying? Absolutely not. Bullying takes many forms, and depending on the personality of the child and the type of bullying, the best response might be very different.

When considering the problem of bullying in your child's life, it's important to take a stand on bullying based logically and biblically and not on emotions. There's nothing like a threat to my children to knock me down a peg or two on the maturity ladder. To make a decision that will be in my child's best interest in the long-run means I might have to set my fears aside.

Is Bullying a Problem?

Bullying is a serious problem in any child's life. Statistics are all over the board on the prevalence of the problem. Depending on your definition of bullying, it can affect up to 90 percent of fourth through eighth grade students, according to the American Psychological Association.

Bullying isn't something most children just shrug off. It impacts them deeply and for years to come. If someone bullies your child, he can experience fear, anger, hopelessness with significant personality changes, and withdrawal or depression. We've all watched the news reports of bullied children who grow up to be violent offenders, seeking revenge for their abuse. Bullying over time has devastating effects on people. However, bullying not only affects the one being bullied, it also affects those observing.

Paul Coughlin, author of *No More Jellyfish, Chickens, or Wimps*, believes there is no such thing as an innocent bystander when it comes to bullying. If your child isn't being bullied but observes it happening, she can be affected based on how she responds. If she does nothing, she may experience feelings of guilt and sadness for abandoning someone in need. If she responds inappropriately with aggression or revenge, she could be just as harmful as the bully. Most children don't know how to respond and end up doing nothing.

According to Coughlin, "About 85 percent of all school-based bullying takes place in front of other kids—that gives bullies the emotional high and ego stroke they're seeking. Most bullying would not take place if it weren't for the display of power they want others to witness."[1]

Bullying is a problem that affects everyone involved. No one wins when a bully is allowed to intimidate others. The good news is parents can prepare their children to deal with bullies and to defend the victims of bullies.

What Is Bullying?

It's important to identify how bullying differs from everyday teasing. Not every mean or rude behavior on the part of another child is bullying. Because of this we need to guard against overreacting to normal childhood behavior. That doesn't mean that it is okay when another child teases your daughter, but it doesn't make it bullying.

Elin McCoy, in *What to Do When Kids Are Mean to Your Child*, offers this definition of bullying:

> When trying to distinguish the two (bullying and meanness), it helps to think of a continuum. At one end are those mildly nasty, but pretty typical, behaviors like pushing and shoving, name-calling, teasing, and telling someone you don't want them on your team. At the other end are activities that border on the criminal: slamming someone into a locker, extorting a toy, a lunch, a favorite jacket, or even money, and threatening kids with total isolation from everyone in the class. Somewhere in the middle of this continuum, when one child or a group regularly torments another child psychologically or physically…typical "meanness" becomes bullying.[2]

Not too many years ago, bullies were limited to the playground or a park on the way home from school. Today bullying takes many forms, including cyber-bullying. This can include such things as sending threatening text messages, e-mail, or instant messages. Bullies can post pictures, messages, rumors, and lies in blogs or on websites. A few years ago, a girl in Robbie's class said she started an "I hate Robbie Whitwer" MySpace page. It wasn't the truth, but it worried Robbie nonetheless.

What's a Parent to Do?

Anytime our child says he is being bullied, we should take it seriously. Take the time to sit down in a quiet setting with your child to talk through what's going on. Allow your child to talk uninterrupted about the problem. Show compassion and empathy, but not anger.

Let your child know you take his comments very seriously but don't overreact. Share your own experiences to let your child know she isn't alone. Then ask specifics. Find out as many details as you can about the bullying. Here are some questions to ask:

- How long has it been going on?
- Where did it happen?
- Does any other adult know?
- Where are the adults when it's happening?
- Did any other children witness the bullying?

Write down all the details and if there is any damage to your child's belongings. If your child is injured in any way, take a photo. It's best to do this without making a big deal in front of your child. Do it discreetly to avoid your child clamming up.

What you do next depends on the extent and the location of the offense. If something criminal happened, you have a responsibility to report it to the police. If it happened at a school, library, after-school program, or other public place, you should report it to those authorities. If the offense was relatively minor, you can help your child deal with it one-on-one and, with God's help, take steps now to avoid any further bullying.

Who Will Be a Victim of Bullying?

Victims of bullies aren't who you might think they are. They don't all wear glasses, have a weight problem, or keep their noses in books. But there are commonalities among bully victims. By knowing them, you can help your child be better prepared in social settings.

According to Paul Coughlin, "Bully victims often come from overprotective homes where they get little if any practice handling conflict. As a result they have little, if any, confidence in their ability to negotiate the world on their own. Overprotection prevents them from learning the skills necessary to avoid exploitation."[3]

In fact Coughlin developed a list of common traits of bully victims, and it has much more to do with the child's inability to set healthy boundaries regarding how he wants to be treated by others than any physical attributes. The list includes the following characteristics:

- They give in too quickly to the demands of others.

- They cry, cower, and overreact.

- They refuse to defend themselves, which is disliked by all peers.

- They are overly sensitive to good-natured teasing.

- They radiate low self-confidence and have a submissive nature.

- They don't get along socially with their peers.

This description of a bullying victim is very similar to that of a child with overprotective parents. Teachers, coaches, and volunteers can spot these children in an instant because a parent is hovering somewhere close by. At the sign of a problem, Mom or Dad steps in to save the day. Thus, the child lacks the experience necessary to be an independent problem solver.

Just this summer at our church's junior camp (grades three through six), the children's ministry leaders (who are good friends of ours) shared their frustration in the overwhelming number of children who couldn't deal with conflict on their own. These children cried, complained to any adult who would listen, and basically alienated themselves from others. The children's behavior was draining on the adults and annoying to those children who were just trying to have a great camp experience.

Based on this information, it would seem that parents actually can have a significant impact on preparing their children to deal well with others and even protecting their children from bullies.

Bully-Proof Your Child

Some common practices can help you bully-proof your child. I think most parents would agree that it's better to be proactive than reactive when it comes to bullies. Most experts agree on the following:

- *Connect with friends.* Having a group of true friends is one of the best defenses against bullies. True friends affirm your child's worth and value. True friends will stick up for your child in a difficult situation.

- *Be direct.* Teach your child to be honest and direct about what she wants or needs. This is a good training ground for setting healthy boundaries.

- *Respond calmly to a situation.* When your child is hurt or offended, teach him to respond calmly rather than give in to emotions and react. Taking a minute to think through a situation and formulate a response will help your child learn self-control and teach him relationship-building skills.

- *Stand up for yourself.* As your child learns her worth is based on her position as a child of God, she begins to see her value. No one has the right to intimidate her or her friends. There should be a sense of holy justice that rises up in us when we understand that fact. When someone bullies your child, she has the right and the responsibility to tell the bully to stop.

- *Be assertive, not aggressive.* Teach your child the difference between standing up for what is right and retaliating. As Christians we follow a moral code of how to treat each other, given to us by a holy God. We have the right to speak out against injustice. Our God cares for the oppressed and seeks justice on their behalf (Psalm 9:8-10).

- *Teach social skills.* We all need to learn how to live in community with others. If you see your child has a difficult time relating to children her own age, spend some time going over rules of common courtesy.

When to Tell Someone in Authority

Most children have an unwritten rule of silence and unfortunately seldom report bullying. After all, it's embarrassing to admit someone pushed you around. Plus many children are scolded for tattling and are unsure about whether this fits that definition or not. However, bullying is an unfair imbalance of power, and for it to stop, children must understand what bullying is and be invited to tell an adult. Hopefully you've created an atmosphere of openness in your home, and your child will tell you the truth. If not it's never too late to start.

If bullying happens at school, you should report it immediately. Even if your child insists the teachers won't do anything about it, report the incident. If you get little to no response at the first level you address, move up the hierarchy of authority until someone responds. Schools that aggressively address the issue of bullying have experienced great success.

There isn't one parent of a bullied and injured child who isn't praying for someone to have the moral courage to do something about bullying. If you see a need in your community for someone to do something, maybe God is calling you.

Developing Moral Courage

While writing this chapter, I will admit I've altered my opinion about how to respond to bullies. By researching the issue from different standpoints, I've taken a more assertive stand. I believe bullies have influence and power beyond the back alley and have frightened millions into submission without us knowing it. Fear for my safety and my children's safety led me to a position of relative passivity, which I've now learned only fosters an environment where bullying flourishes.

As I've read literature and reviewed websites about dealing with bullies, there's a common thread of "ignore it and it will go away." I've read professional advice that encourages you to agree with the bully when he or she teases you. Other advice says to never defend yourself with physical force no matter what the bully does to you.

I guess that would be a great response if it worked. But apparently it doesn't. Dr. Dan Olweus, author of *Bullying at School: What We Know and What We Can Do*, describes the typical victim as someone who makes no assertive response to the aggression. When there is no response, it happens again.

Teaching your child to ignore *teasing* is a good response. Yet, ignoring a true bully won't always stop the torment. There may be a time when your child needs to stand his ground and confront the bully, just as David did.

I grew up loving the story of David and Goliath. I read the story out of the Little Golden Books, and Sunday school teachers retold the drama using flannel boards. I can almost picture little David standing his ground in front of the giant Goliath with only a slingshot, while the entire Israelite army quaked in fear. Woosh, woosh, woosh, around his head the slingshot swung. With a strong arm, David let the stone fly and bam! The giant fell, and David was victorious.

What a great story! But is it a story to be left in the history books, or are we to learn anything from David's example? As I read the passage in 1 Samuel 17, a few things jumped out at me. First, David wasn't planning to get in a fight that day. He was just an errand boy sent to deliver food to his brothers and report to their father. So truly he was just a bystander. But as David neared the front lines, he quickly realized what was happening. He heard the taunts of Goliath and got drawn into the situation. Something within David's heart started to stir, maybe a righteous anger. David tried to get someone to answer his questions about this bully. He wanted to know what was going to be done about this man.

David finally asked in exasperation: "Who is this uncircumcised Philistine that he should defy the armies of the living God?" David's anger didn't flare because he or his brothers were being threatened. His anger burned because someone dared to threaten and defy those chosen by his God.

When the trained professionals wouldn't step forward, David—confident of his God's power and protection—spurned armor and helmet, put five stones in his shepherd's bag, and approached the bully. Calmly David said to Goliath, "You come against me with sword and spear and javelin, but I come against you in the name of the LORD Almighty, the God of the armies of Israel, whom you have defied" (1 Samuel 17:45). With only one stone, David felled the giant and defeated the Philistine army.

We could write off the courage of David as a legend to be enjoyed but not applied to our lives today except for two biblical truths. First, David was a man after God's heart (Acts 13:22), and second, God doesn't change (Malachi 3:6).

Although Jesus calls us to a life of forgiveness and compassion, even He didn't tolerate those who dishonored God's holy temple. With righteous indignation, Jesus turned over tables and drove out money changers and those who were selling doves within the walls of the temple, accusing them of turning His father's house into "a den of robbers" (Mark 11:17).

Yes, Jesus calls us to "turn the other cheek," but we do that out of our own choice and will, not because of fear. Jesus could have called down a thousand angels to protect Him from being crucified, but He willingly laid down His life. Jesus states this in His own words, "The reason my Father loves me is that I lay down my life—only to take it up again. No one takes it from me, but I lay it down of my own accord. I have authority to lay it down and authority to take it up again. This command I received from my Father" (John 10:17-18).

The Bible records stories of men and women with moral courage. These individuals knew what was right and were willing to take a stand. They weren't perfect, but the heroes of our faith saw injustice as more than a personal offense—they saw it as an offense against God.

As it becomes easier to settle into a life of ambiguity, our children are finding it harder and harder to summon moral outrage about anything. Perhaps that's because many adults seldom experience righteous indignation. The question begs to be asked: Are we raising a generation who will tolerate offenses against those beloved by God based on our own fear?

The Bottom Line About Bullying

Today a challenge is set before us as parents to raise men and women who will stand for what is right. We can't learn moral courage from a book. We can only learn it by being brave once—then doing it again. Bravery takes practice because it isn't something most people are born with. Ralph Waldo Emerson said, "A hero is no braver than an ordinary man, but he is brave five minutes longer."

Sometimes bravery means turning the other cheek. But that's only bravery when you submit willingly. Our children are being taught by some to submit in fear to bullies. Cowardice isn't a godly trait because the one caught up in it simply stands by and lets wrong-doing perpetuate itself.

The bottom line is we have the responsibility to protect our children. Pray about what this means in your situation but don't ignore the problem. Without fail, everyone who has ignored bullying regrets it. As Christians we can be assertive without being aggressive. We can defend ourselves without seeking revenge. We can stand up for the human rights of others. We can stand against injustice. And we can stand alongside David in outrage at the attack on God's people. That's moral courage in the making.

Memory Verses

Be on guard. Stand firm in the faith.
Be courageous. Be strong.

1 CORINTHIANS 16:13 NLT

He will judge the world in righteousness; he will
govern the peoples with justice. The LORD is a refuge
for the oppressed, a stronghold in times of trouble.
Those who know your name will trust in you, for you,
LORD, have never forsaken those who seek you.

PSALM 9: 8-10

*Do not withhold good from those who deserve
it, when it is in your power to act.*

PROVERBS 3:27

*But those who hope in the LORD will renew their
strength. They will soar on wings like eagles; they will run
and not grow weary, they will walk and not be faint.*

ISAIAH 40:31

*Do not spread false reports. Do not help a
wicked man by being a malicious witness. Do
not follow the crowd in doing wrong.*

EXODUS 23:1-2

Encouraging Words

*Don't hit at all if it is honorably possible
to avoid hitting, but never hit soft.*

—THEODORE ROOSEVELT

*Moral excellence comes about as a result of habit.
We become just by doing just acts, temperate by
doing temperate acts, brave by doing brave acts.*

—ARISTOTLE

Courage is fire, and bullying is smoke.

—BENJAMIN DISRAELI

*Heroes are people who rise to the
occasion and slip quietly away.*

—TOM BROKAW

Discussion or Journal Questions

1. Do you remember a time when you were bullied or observed someone else being bullied? Describe your emotions.

2. Why do you think bullies have power over other people?

3. How has fear of others (what they will say or do) ever kept you from doing something you wanted to do?

4. What are some ways parents overprotect their children?

5. How does overprotecting a child keep him or her from learning coping skills?

6. Why are bystanders never innocent victims?

7. What long-term problems can arise when someone allows bullying to occur?

8. What should a Christian's response be to injustice?

9. What are some ways to increase courage?

10. Identify some steps you can take now to bully-proof your children.

Chapter Fourteen

Caring for a Child with a Physical Difference

There was a crooked man…

My initial vision for this book was to deal with the challenges that children face every day. While I haven't been able to address them all, I hoped to hit the most common. You've worked your way through this book and are now facing what may seem like quite a deviation from that theme. It's likely that you picked up this book specifically because your child doesn't need professional help. You just needed to hear from people who have walked a bit farther down the road of parenting than you and were willing to share their successes.

However, every day a normal child in a normal household on a normal street has something abnormal happen. Whether it started at birth, came on in preschool, or happened in a car accident, parents around the world have their normal lives turned upside down. Their precious child is no longer perfect.

"Something is wrong," the doctor says. "Your child has… He will probably never…" the surgeon agrees. Mom looks at Dad, wondering what went wrong. She did everything right during pregnancy, didn't she? He watched over his daughter like a hawk. How could this have happened?

They didn't sign up for this lot in life, and neither did their child. But in the span of a heartbeat, they have been assigned the remarkable task of caring for a child with a physical difference or disability. It can happen to me, and it can happen to you. It can happen to someone we love and someone who lives next door.

That's why I wanted to address this topic—because everyone faces a challenge of some kind and normal is only based on statistics. Children are just children, and their parents are just parents.

Because each diagnosis brings with it a unique set of needs, it would be presumptuous of me to try to cover the depth and breadth of cares that children and parents face. However, I hope that in sharing the stories of two friends of mine, you will be encouraged.

They both have wisdom to share that can apply to every parent. I'm confident that the truths God revealed to them over the years will benefit you. I have learned much in listening to their stories and have gained an increased appreciation for every parent who has walked a similar path.

Jordan's Story

Jordan was a beautiful, healthy baby. The firstborn son of two caring parents, he was deeply loved. His mother, Sue Eickman, was an elementary school teacher, who enjoyed every detail of parenting and took special enjoyment in studying her son's physical development. Thankfully Jordan excelled in every way.

The first few months were exciting and an answer to their prayers. Jordan was a charming baby and a delight to everyone. However, at about the fifth month of Jordan's life, just as he was starting to eat rice cereal and spit out pureed green beans, Sue and her husband, Larry, noticed something distressing about their son. Maybe it was nothing, but it seemed odd.

They started to realize that Jordan didn't respond to any of the household noises. While most parents are thankful that the phone ringing doesn't wake their child from a nap, this was a growing cause of concern. Could their baby even hear the noise? Over the next weeks, they decided to do some tests of their own. A pot was hit with a spoon. Keys were rattled. They called Jordan's name when he was looking out the window. No response.

The reality dawned on Sue and Larry. Their son couldn't hear. The first stop was Jordan's pediatrician, who wasn't concerned. Basically he told them they were being overprotective, first-time parents. This didn't sit well with Sue and Larry whose instincts were telling them otherwise.

With no formal diagnosis at hand and not willing to wait, the Eickmans enrolled Jordan in a private child development center dealing with children of different disabilities. By this time Jordan was experiencing other developmental delays, so the program helped. Although the staff hadn't dealt with a deaf baby, they offered excellent care.

By the time Jordan was 12 months old, the Eickmans were ready to push for a formal diagnosis. A trip to the local ear, nose, and throat doctor was a disaster, and Sue petitioned the pediatrician for a referral to a specialist. The insurance company granted the referral, and Sue and Larry packed up baby Jordan for a trip to Chicago.

The doctor took Jordan behind closed doors for the testing, which included sedation to test the extent of his hearing loss. When the doctor returned to the waiting room holding baby Jordan, he only confirmed what Sue and Larry already knew—Jordan was profoundly deaf.

As the doctor looked at these two devoted parents, he spoke words that Sue and Larry never forgot—words that became a catalyst for the coming years: "Your goal now is to get this child educated."

Educating Jordan became Sue's full-time occupation and joy. Sue explains, "We had this urgency to learn everything we could about deafness. Then we wanted to know what we were going to do with this child."

Some family members started taking sign language classes, including Jordan's grandparents. Sue then got on the phone and called everyone she could think of. One friend, who lived in a different town, suggested she call the local school district. That piece of advice turned out to be a nugget of gold because the school subcontracted with an organization that sent a parent and infant specialist to the house every week. This specialist was a lifeline for the Eickmans, and Jordan thrived.

As Jordan approached first grade, Sue and Larry were faced with the decision of how to best formally educate their son. By this time Jordan was exhibiting a high intelligence and was absorbing every learning experience with enthusiasm. Most parents of deaf children were sending their elementary-aged kids to full-time residential programs. But this didn't appeal to the Eickmans who were committed to being part of their son's education. They started their research again and discovered a day school for the deaf in Phoenix.

Seeing this as God's answer to their prayers, they moved to Phoenix, and Jordan started school. He quickly excelled in all areas, and teachers recommended him for the gifted program. The Eickmans creatively used the public school system for some of the gifted programming and the school for the deaf for certain classes and socialization. In the early elementary grades when an interpreter wasn't available, Sue interpreted in the classroom for her son. Upon graduation from high school, Jordan entered college and earned a bachelor of arts degree in cultural geography.

Jordan then began a master's program, but during that first year he applied for and received the British Marshall scholarship. He chose the University of Bristol in England because of their deaf studies program and initially began to study for a master's of philosophy (MPhil). He then earned an upgrade to enter and complete the doctoral program there.

Jordan's story of success continues. He currently is an assistant professor at the Department of Deaf Studies at California State University, Northridge, working toward earning tenure. His other accomplishments extend beyond the classroom and include being a three-time Deaflympics athlete in water polo and the current director of United States Deaf Water Polo, the deaf national sports organization responsible for deaf water polo.

Hannah's Story

Barb and Tim Frey had prayed for a baby, but after four years of trying, they were wondering if it would ever happen. So Barb was surprised when a friend called to share a message from God that he'd received during his prayer time. God told this friend that Barb would get pregnant, deliver a baby, and her name would be Hannah. Two months later, Barb was pregnant.

The pregnancy was normal, and the baby was healthy. During the labor and delivery though, things were very difficult. Hannah was born safely, but within six hours after delivery, Barb started experiencing seizures due to undetected preeclampsia. The doctors were able to stop the seizures and told Barb that 2 percent of women will have this condition during delivery, but only a small percentage of those will have a seizure disorder for life. Unfortunately Barb was one of those women.

On the day the hospital staff was preparing to release Barb, she suffered a grand mal seizure. This sent her down the path to neurological specialists and heavy medication. Barb was a new mother, and fear and worry gripped her constantly. How would she parent this child? Thanks to good friends and family, Barb got through those first months, and life returned to a form of normal. But the fear of another seizure was always with her, and care for her precious baby was of top concern.

Hannah developed normally, and within a few years, healthy baby sister Naomi joined the family. In the midst of Barb's concern over her health and fear for the pregnancy with Naomi, Barb started noticing that Hannah was experiencing what she labeled the "terrible twos." Where Hannah used to be obedient, she now ignored her mother's requests. Barb also noticed Hannah's communication skills, which had always been delayed, were now even more challenging. Barb chalked this up to normal childhood rebellion on Hannah's part.

It wasn't until a friend babysat Hannah that Barb started putting things together. When Barb arrived to pick up Hannah, the friend said, "I don't think Hannah's hearing me. Hannah was in the corner of the yard where all the other kids were playing, and I called the kids for lunch. All the other children came. It wasn't like Hannah looked at me and made a choice. She didn't hear me."

Barb and Tim started testing Hannah at home by setting up scenarios, and the same thing happened. They took their toddler to an ears, nose, and throat doctor, whom they are convinced God had set in place long before they knew they had a need. This same doctor also had an audiology clinic at an off-site location. He referred the Freys to the clinic, and very quickly the staff discovered Hannah had a hearing loss in the moderate to severe range in both ears. Based on Hannah's history and normal development up to age two, the doctor suggested that, at some point in the past year, something had malfunctioned or misfired and damaged her hearing.

The Freys felt as if they were in a whirlwind and flying by the seat of their pants with this diagnosis. They already lived in Phoenix and knew about the day school for the deaf, although that didn't seem like the right decision for their family. So Barb and Tim started their own search for options. The audiology clinic helped and told them about a nonprofit organization that taught hearing impaired people, even profoundly deaf people, to speak.

They contacted the organization, did their research, and decided to give it a try. Although it was tough at times and they faced much harsh judgment for their decision to not learn sign language, the Freys were confident in their decision to do what they could to mainstream Hannah. Their decision proved to be the right one for Hannah. She excelled in the program and, with a combination of training and hearing aids, participates in all activities without a translator.

Hannah graduated from high school, lettering in academics all four years. She's now in college and training to be a graphic artist. Although Hannah has faced challenges due to her hearing loss, God is still leading Hannah to fulfill her dreams.

Do What's Best for Your Child

Two different parents, two unique children, and one similar (though not exact) issue of deafness—these two sets of families chose very different paths for their children, and each was the right choice.

Although these stories deal with hearing loss, similar stories are told around the world of children with different diagnoses, from mild to severe. Every day parents look a doctor in the face and hear a diagnosis for their precious child. Immediately they must face an array of doctors and decisions. Which path is right for their child? Is there even a right and wrong? How can you make a wise decision when you are struggling with so many emotions yourself?

Sue and Larry and Barb and Tim are outstanding examples of parents who submitted their wills to God, prayed fervently for direction, and followed that guidance despite what others around them were doing. In both instances they did what was best for their child and their family.

Neither couple settled for the first and most obvious option for their child. They weren't content to face a single path to follow. So they pushed, dug, and persisted until they uncovered a variety of choices. Then despite pressure from friends or family, they made decisions that were best for their children.

The learning curve was steep for both families. After all, how do you know what you don't know? In the midst of sorting out differing medical, social, educational, and emotional advice from professionals, they had to factor in advice from others. Sometimes it was well-meaning advice, and sometimes it was judgmental. No matter where the advice originated, it was important to the parents of Jordan and Hannah to filter it through God's wisdom and then feel confident in making the best decision without regrets.

Barb told me that she had to learn to trust her instincts. "I had a lot of common sense, but I didn't know it was okay to think the way I was thinking. Most parents know what's best for their child, and they need courage to pursue that course. Parents need affirmation to trust their instincts."

The truth is God has chosen you as the parent of your child for a reason. It was not a mistake. He trusts you with a precious life. It doesn't matter what others are doing for their children—God wants you to make the decisions for your child.

After the shock had worn off and the sadness diminished, both parents knew what they had to do: Zero in on their children's needs and do whatever it took to meet them.

Praying for God's Best

It didn't hit me until after spending time with Sue and Barb, that both women and their husbands are prayer warriors. Not only are they devoted to personal prayer, but they are actively involved in the leadership of different prayer ministries at our church. They have experienced God's power through prayer. Now they are passionate about praying for others.

At one point God gave Barb a vision of stepping stones. God seemed to be telling her, "You may be in a difficult place now, but it's a good place. You are learning things. But I have readied something better for you. Just step off the stone." As Barb prayed about that vision, God revealed a monumental truth to her: God wanted the best for Hannah. God's best might be to restore her hearing, but it might be something else.

Praying for God's best for our children changes our attitude. It takes us from a temporal viewpoint to a place where eternity seems real. As we consider God's best, the disappointment over the world's (and our) expectations for our children fades away. Instead, God's peace covers us and brings hope.

As we read the stories of Jesus healing men and women, we can be confident that God longs to restore bodies to full health. But that wasn't Jesus' only goal. His goal was to bring life. John 10:10-11 (NASB) records Jesus' words, "I came that they may have life, and have it abundantly. I am the good shepherd; the good shepherd lays down His life for the sheep."

Yes, our physical life here on earth is important, but it's not God's best. God's best is life with Him for eternity. But while we are here, we will pray for God's best right now and trust His answers.

Sue is very clear on the two best things she did for Jordan—pray and trust God. "Everything boils down to trusting God with what you have been given, seeking the Lord's advice and counsel, and putting your trust in Him. That is the bottom line."

Focus on Opportunities

The words of the doctor in Chicago echoed in the ears of Sue and Larry: "Your goal now is to get this child educated." They took that advice to heart and set out to expose their son to every experience possible. Sue looked at everything as a learning experience. Although Jordan was missing his hearing, he still had other senses that needed stimulation. So Sue and Larry took him to play in the sandbox. They went to the zoo, the parade, the museum, and the cheese factory. They bought finger paints, and they worked together in the garden. Sue became Jordan's enthusiastic teacher, opening up the world to her son.

Teaching Jordan through signing was part of preparing him to fully explore every opportunity available. Sue and Larry used Signed English (not a signed language but a system for signing English) with the intention to teach Jordan English literacy skills. They later learned that American Sign Language (ASL) is the best way to teach deaf children language and English literacy skills. They also learned that Jordan was one of the "exceptions" who would have learned English literacy skills through either ASL or Signed English.

The significance here is that they chose a signed modality over an entirely oral method of communication. This allowed Jordan to communicate his thoughts and have rich and meaningful conversations with others. Communication is critical to relationships, and today Jordan believes it is necessary for all deaf children and those who love them to learn ASL

Sue said, "We were so hungry with what we could do with our son. He wasn't going to learn like a hearing child through the ears—he was going to learn through his eyes. We needed to figure out what we could do to give Jordan every opportunity a hearing child would have." Jordan's natural curiosity was fed, and his mind brightened with each experience. He longed for more, and Sue figured out how to create opportunities. Instead of protecting her son from the questions and stares they would receive while signing, she prepared Jordan to be a part of the world.

Barb and Tim made similar choices. Barb commented, "We never treated her like she was different. In fact sometimes she'd have to remind me that she couldn't hear clearly. We just never set limitations on her."

What a gift to any child—parents who don't focus on the limitations, only the opportunities.

Identify Their Gifts

Even though children may have limitations in one area, God has certainly gifted them in others. In chapter 11, I covered the importance of identifying personal strengths and touched on spiritual gifts. It is even more important that we explore this with our children who have physical limitations. It is very possible your child will have above average strengths in verbal or written skills. Or perhaps your child is gifted socially or in the area of compassion.

Years ago I had a friend who was blind. She lived independently and was in school to become a massage therapist. What always amazed me was her ability to see into the heart of someone. Within a short time of knowing her, I felt as if we were best friends. She had a gift of listening and intuitively knew how to skim past the surface to dive into the depth of any matter. God has blessed her abundantly in the area of interpersonal communications.

What gifts does your child have?

Be Flexible

When parenting a child, there is usually no rulebook to follow. Many times it's trial and error. As Sue learned, being flexible is the key to success. "Being flexible was really key to dealing with our situation. If something doesn't work out, fit, mesh, or just plain doesn't seem right, be flexible enough to go back to the drawing board, even if it means starting from scratch."

This doesn't mean you've failed. It just means you're willing to keep trying until you find greater success. A quote from Douglas MacArthur sums it up nicely. "We are not retreating—we are advancing in another direction."

List Your Blessings

In the midst of the frustrations, pain, and heartbreak, take some time to list your blessings. Sue and Larry created a blessing box to capture the blessings they might overlook in the demands of everyday life. They recorded the big blessings God gave their son, their family, and themselves on little slips of paper.

This blessing box reminded them to be thankful for God's mercy and care. Even though at times it seemed they had been given a difficult road to travel, they knew God was with them.

The Eickmans are living out the apostle Paul's commandment to the believers in Colossians 4:2, "Devote yourselves to prayer, being watchful and thankful." They are truly examples of parents who looked to God for direction and obeyed.

God Has a Plan

One of the most heartbreaking questions a parent will ever hear is "Why did God make me this way?" or "Why did God let this happen?"

Barb has responded with wisdom and grace when those words were spoken. Her answer is simple but profound: "What I know is that God has a plan for you. It's not going to be easy, but God will be with you. It's all we have, but it's enough."

Memory Verses

*"For I know the plans I have for you," declares
the LORD, "plans to prosper you and not to harm
you, plans to give you hope and a future."*

JEREMIAH 29:11

*The LORD looks down from heaven on the sons of men to
see if there are any who understand, any who seek God.*

PSALM 14:2

Our God is in the heavens; he does whatever he pleases.

PSALM 115:3 RSV

But he was wounded for our transgressions, he was bruised for our iniquities; upon him was the chastisement that made us whole, and with his stripes we are healed.

ISAIAH 53:5 RSV

Do not be anxious about anything, but in everything, by prayer and petition, with thanksgiving, present your requests to God. And the peace of God, which transcends all understanding, will guard your hearts and your minds in Christ Jesus.

PHILIPPIANS 4:6-7

Encouraging Words

God's answers are wiser than our prayers.

—UNKNOWN

I thank God for my handicaps, for, through them, I have found myself, my work, and my God.

—HELEN KELLER

Not what we say about our blessings, but how we use them, is the true measure of our thanksgiving.

—W.T. PURKISER

Most of the important things in the world have been accomplished by people who have kept on trying when there seemed to be no help at all.

—DALE CARNEGIE

God, who foresaw your tribulation, has specially armed
you to go through it, not without pain but without stain.

—C.S. Lewis

Discussion or Journal Questions

1. Before your child was born, did you have hopes and dreams for him or her? What were they?

2. Read Hebrews 13:5. What is God's promise to us in this verse? What does this mean during difficult times?

3. Read Philippians 4:6-7. What types of things does God invite us to pray about?

4. Is there anything in your child's life that you have neglected to pray about? Make a list of these things and commit to praying about them in the coming week.

5. What should accompany our prayers and petitions? Is there anything in your life you would like to thank God for now? Make another list if that would be helpful.

6. What is God's promise to us if we present our requests to Him with thanksgiving? Describe what peace feels like.

7. What are your greatest fears regarding your child?

8. If you could identify God's best for your life, what would it look like? Describe.

9. Think about your child's natural gifts and talents. Make a list of some of his or her God-given gifts that you can nurture and encourage.

Chapter Fifteen

When Your Child Learns Differently

...and hide his head under his wing, poor thing.

Some kids' number one stress factor in life is school. School stresses some kids out more than parents, siblings, mean people, or sports. Even the brightest and most motivated children worry about school from time to time. So for a moment, imagine how it must feel for a child who struggles with learning.

What if the letters on the page seemed to dance around in front of you? What if everyone else understood the teacher's directions, but they got jumbled up somewhere between your ears and your brain? What if everyone else in the class seemed to know how to do the worksheet, but you had been looking out the window and wondering what it would be like to fly when the teacher explained it.

In 2006, the National Center for Health Statistics indicated that 15 percent of children aged 3 to 17 had some type of learning difficulty.[1] I imagine the actual numbers are much higher if we factored in those children whose learning challenges were undiagnosed. Unfortunately diagnosing a learning difficulty early is hard.

If a child's learning issues were isolated from other behaviors and had clear-cut edges, maybe a parent could easily call in a specialist. Then with one test she could diagnose and treat the child. But that's not how learning differences work. A child with a learning difficulty doesn't normally just waltz out of school to a perfect life. That learning issue goes with him and has the potential to affect almost every other area of his life.

Because the first symptoms of a learning difficulty aren't always associated with learning, it's difficult for parents to diagnose it early. It is as if you know you have a bug bite somewhere on your leg, but your whole leg itches, so you can't isolate it. Your child can't tell you what's going on, and the frustration often swells over into other areas, confusing the real issue at hand.

Neither my husband nor I have any diagnosed learning disabilities in our families. In fact we both come from families filled with professional educators, from professors at Harvard to first grade teachers. Almost everyone in our family is college educated. So when our son started struggling in school, we were unprepared to deal with it. That never happened in our families. In fact we didn't acknowledge there was a real problem for a few years, until we could no longer make any excuses.

I've shared many of my family's struggles throughout the book, but this has been the most difficult by far. My children have grown past other challenges they have faced, hopefully better prepared for the next time. But this one is different. This one had the potential to be much more damaging when we first dealt with it—and still does have potential for damage.

This has been a hard road to walk, and my husband and I have made lots of mistakes. I'll share some of those as I tell our story. But thanks to the wisdom of God, teachers, counselors, and family members, we've also experienced success. This story isn't finished. There are many more chapters to live. Let me bring you up to date and share what we've learned so far. I pray that our experience will help your child or someone you love. At the very least, I want you to know you are not alone. There is always a rainbow after the storm. That's a promise we can count on!

Joshua's Story

"Joshua! Stop!"

"Joshua, don't touch that!"

"Joshua, come back here!"

Within minutes of being anywhere—the doctor's waiting room,

McDonald's play area, or a store—everyone knew my son's name. When he was a toddler, keeping track of him exhausted me. Even at a friend's house with other children around, he didn't sit and play. He explored. Which, of course, meant that I trailed behind him.

Relief flooded my mind and body the minute we walked in our front door. At least there I knew we'd covered every outlet, removed every chemical from reach, and raised every knickknack. Even at home, however, Joshua kept busy.

Nothing held his attention for very long except Barney on TV and having a book read to him. Because Joshua had such a short attention span, I was his chief entertainer. If we weren't playing or reading together, I provided him with something to do. Those early years were trying, especially after the next two boys joined the family.

Although Joshua demanded much of me physically, his personality radiated joy. His sweet attitude drew others to him immediately. As he grew, he never had the "terrible" twos or the "Mine!" attitude. He loved his little brothers and shared everything he had. Nothing could ruffle his sunny disposition.

Joshua's first exposures to formal teaching were at Sunday school and vacation Bible school, where I heard similar comments. They all went something like this, "Joshua is in his own little world, but somehow he always knows the answers."

Kindergarten and First Grade

Joshua attended preschool and kindergarten in small Christian schools. He excelled in his language skills and learned to read with ease. He was cooperative, friendly, and helpful. There were no noticeable learning or behavior problems until first grade.

The first grade Joshua attended was in the same Christian school as his kindergarten class. In fact that year the school decided to start an elementary school, and they planned to grow the school one grade at a time. They hoped the children in this first grade class would continue. It was a wonderful setting for our son. The nine children in the classroom all knew each other from kindergarten, and we hoped the teacher's personal attention would accelerate learning. My husband and I believed it would be a wonderful experience for our son, who was showing signs of being very bright.

However, very soon after the start of school, I started getting notes from the teacher. They typically read something like this: "Joshua whistled in class today. I would ask him to stop, and he would. Then soon after he would start again. Every time I asked him to stop, he was very agreeable, but then the whistling would begin again."

If it wasn't whistling, it was rocking back in his chair, playing with his pencils, or tapping on his desk. It was always something. As a conscientious mother, I encouraged her notes. I wanted to know what was happening in the classroom and support the teacher at home by affirming correct behavior. Josh and I would have long talks (too long for a six-year-old) about his behavior. He knew he shouldn't whistle, rock, or tap, and he agreed, with all the sincerity he could muster, that he would stop.

The next day, however, another note was stuck in his take-home folder. Every day when I saw that slip of paper, I grew more and more upset. Every afternoon the discussions continued, and my little boy grew more and more discouraged. "Why?" I'd ask repeatedly. "I don't know," he'd answer over and over. Talking did no good, so I started threatening a negative consequence if I got a note. The notes continued. He wasn't argumentative, defiant, or mean, so I couldn't understand why he would consistently disobey his teacher and parents in class.

The situation took its toll on Joshua. My joyful little son was turning into a fearful and worried child. Finally I'd had enough of the afternoon talks, the punishments, and notes. I didn't know what was motivating Joshua to disobey, but I saw him changing, and that was concerning. That afternoon I asked to speak to the teacher privately and requested that the notes stop. I didn't want to hear about every little thing Joshua did wrong. If there was something major, I wanted to hear, but it was time to stop reporting on his every move.

Instead of telling me about what Joshua did wrong, I asked her to tell me what he did right. Then I told Josh, "When I get a good report from the teacher, I will have a special treat for you at home." Within a day Joshua's behavior started changing. Reward was a much more effective motivator than punishment. While this didn't stop his repetitive behavior, he got through the rest of the year without much incident. Joshua continued to do well in school and was above average in all areas of academics.

Second Grade

The next summer our family moved from Phoenix to North Carolina. In Phoenix I had been working part-time to pay for the private school. But in North Carolina, we decided I would stay home and put the boys in the public school. Thankfully we moved to a high achieving school district where the educational standard was even higher than in the private school back in Phoenix.

Halfway into the school year, the teacher contacted me with some concerns about Joshua's inattention. A large part of learning in her classroom happened in independent centers. For part of the day, the children rotated from one center to another, tackling a math project in one or a science project in another. The teacher observed Joshua having trouble staying on task during this time.

The teacher was a kind woman and spoke with true compassion for Joshua. Because of her gentle approach and concern for Joshua's learning, I was open to her suggestion that perhaps we should have Joshua screened for a learning problem. His grades weren't suffering then, but she was concerned about third grade, where the academic demands would markedly increase.

Deep in my heart, I knew something was different about Joshua. I'd sat in enough groups of children to know my son stood out. My husband and I talked about the testing and agreed to have it done. We filled out questionnaires, and so did the teacher. Then the school psychologist observed Josh several times in the classroom. When the psychologist finished the report, the school administrators scheduled a meeting with all Joshua's teachers to discuss the results.

In the meantime, I researched ADHD, attention deficit/hyperactivity disorder. I checked out some books from the library and took the questionnaires included in the chapters. I was somewhat comforted when Joshua didn't seem to have enough of the characteristics to qualify for an ADHD diagnosis. We'd seen none of the aggressive qualities normally associated with the disorder. He was kind, respectful, agreeable, and emotionally happy. I was sure we would get to that meeting and find out Joshua would grow out of these symptoms.

But that's not what happened. The psychologist agreed that Joshua didn't have many of the common symptoms of ADHD, but the ones he did have ranked off the charts. When she told us Joshua was off-task 85 percent of the time in math, along with other significantly atypical results in a few categories, we were astounded. Joshua appeared to have ADHD. However, to confirm their suspicions, he would need a physician's official diagnosis.

What Next?

Hearing my son discussed in specialized terms rattled me. My vocabulary didn't include words like *atypical* and *off-task*, and I left that meeting with a sick feeling in my stomach. Was my son abnormal? Would he be able to keep up as school increased in difficulty? Had we started down a path with no return?

Questions and worries kept me awake at night. I knew no one whose child had this problem but plenty of people with advice. Before this the only information I had about ADHD came from the media, which regularly included news reports indicating an overdiagnosis of the condition by parents and educators who didn't want to deal with the real problem of an undisciplined child. Was the ADHD label an easy answer to lazy parenting?

Others feared that labeling a child would haunt him for years. Maybe we should act as if the screening never happened. After all, we still had to visit the doctor for confirmation.

Options overwhelmed us. After doing research and talking with well-meaning friends, we narrowed the possibilities down to evaluating Joshua's diet (removing sugar or bread products mainly), taking health food supplements and vitamins, restructuring his day, home-schooling, behavioral coaching, and finally taking medication.

Thankfully the end of the school year bought us time to make a decision. We hoped Josh would grow out of this over the summer. However, third grade put a screeching halt to that optimism.

Third Grade

Soon after the start of third grade, Joshua innocently volunteered two clues that something was stirring. First, he told me the teacher turned his desk around, so he had to get up and walk around it to get a pencil. A few days later, he said the teacher moved his desk near hers.

Anger simmered, threatening to erupt. How dare she embarrass my son like that! I pictured everyone in the classroom turning to watch my little boy be publicly humiliated for his inattention. The worst possible scenarios wrenched my heart, and a grief-like emotion washed over me. I prayed about what to do because I knew my heart was not in a right position. My desire to stomp down to the school and demand changes didn't sound like the right approach.

Soon after learning about these changes with Joshua's desk, the teacher called me in for a meeting. Every defensive bone in my body prepared for attack. But a gentle teacher diffused my anger with her kind and compassionate concern.

"Mrs. Whitwer," she started. "Joshua is a wonderful boy. However, I received a phone call from another parent whose child complained about Joshua distracting her when she was trying to work."

My mind frantically processed the information I had just heard. Even while the teacher spoke, thoughts rampaged through my head: *A child complained to her mother about my son? How could* that *happen? Was the situation worse than I thought?*

The teacher continued, "I had already brought up Joshua's activity level to the third grade teaching team, and we've been trying to help him with a creative approach. I moved him up next to me, and we gave him Q-tips instead of pencils to tap on his desk."

She explained some of the other tactics they tried with some success, to help Josh focus. The biggest concerns now seemed to be alienation from the other children and his difficulty in learning due to inattention. The inattention didn't surprise me, but the fact that Joshua annoyed his classmates shocked me. The teacher repeatedly asked Josh to stop the noise or activity, to which he responded pleasantly. But shortly he resumed the same behavior, unaware he was even doing it.

The time had come to address Joshua's needs head on. Our indecision crash-landed when we learned about the social problems Josh experienced. We figured Joshua could catch up on education if needed, but his self-esteem was our top priority. The thought of our boy sitting alone on the playground galvanized us into action.

We tried several options at home, including natural remedies, changing his diet, and implementing a more structured routine. Finally we tried medication, which was successful for a few years. Then we focused on helping Josh learn coping skills, such as keeping a homework journal and developing good study habits.

Joshua is now a senior in high school. By the time you read this, he will have graduated. I won't try to predict the future, so I can't tell you what Joshua's educational future holds. But I can share a testimony of God's faithfulness in the past.

Self-Esteem Matters Most

God answered our prayers to protect Joshua's self-esteem. I believe God hand picked Joshua's teachers, classmates, neighbors, Sunday school teachers, camp counselors, and youth directors. Starting in North Carolina, God navigated Joshua's path to intersect with loving Christians who saw and encouraged his potential. Josh started playing the bass guitar in fifth grade. By seventh grade he was playing in a youth worship band at church. In ninth grade he started playing guitar and joined a second worship team. Now as a senior, he's been asked to co-lead one of the teams, and he and his brothers started a worship band for a fifth and sixth grade class.

His youth leader identified a seed of leadership and invited Joshua to intern with him this year. Throughout it all, we were ready to make any change necessary to protect Joshua. Thankfully we haven't made any drastic changes. Thanks to God's intervention.

Guard Your Heart Against Judgmental Comments

It seems most people have a strong opinion about how to handle a learning difference. Whether it's pursuing private tutoring, enrolling the child in a Montessori school, private or public school, or home-schooling, people feel passionately about their choice and assume it's best for everyone. They can also find a professional to back up their opinion.

The divide widens when medication is a choice, especially in the Christian community. Mature Christians sit on both sides of the medication fence, both armed with Scripture to defend their position. However, every child has a unique combination of needs, and her parents know that better than anyone.

Unfortunately *someone* will always disagree with whatever decision you make on behalf of your child. If you allow your child to continue in the public school, someone will think you should homeschool. If you homeschool a child with a learning disability, someone will think he should receive professional help. There is no way to please every-one, so focus on pleasing God by being obedient and serving your child's best interest.

I've found the best approach is to diligently research your options, pray continually for your child, submit your will and your pride to God, and then move forward in confidence. Trust God to give you spiritual insight about the right choice. Scripture tells us that God is extravagant with giving wisdom (James 1:5).

If friends or family members fault your decision, agree respectfully not to discuss the subject. Surround yourself with people who support your decision and choose to ignore the judgmental comments of others. This may mean making a difficult change in a current relationship or involvement with a group of people, but having others second-guess or criticize your family's decision will undermine your confidence. Trust me, you will need godly confidence in the years to come.

Be Your Child's Advocate Without Offense

Joshua started singing as soon as he could string a few words together. The boy always has a song in his head or on his lips. Now it is flowing into his ears from his iPod and through his earbuds. We knew God bestowed musical talent upon him at an early age and tried to support this. In first grade Josh took piano lessons at a music academy sponsored by the Christian school he attended.

Focusing on the music was a challenge for Josh. At one point during the year, the teacher actually said, "You are wasting your money." We didn't agree. But we did agree she wasn't the teacher for Joshua. I'm pretty sure she was surprised when, at the recital with approximately 50 children performing, Joshua was the only one who played *and* sang.

People will see your child through different eyes. They may miss the seeds of talent and brilliance you see. They might overlook the tender heart. Others may be blind to your child's potential, which means it is your responsibility to be your child's advocate in all areas.

The key to advocating is to approach the situation with humility and a heart to create a win-win situation. If you believe someone mistreated your child or if tension surrounds the issue, remove any blame from the discussion. Stay away from asking "why?" Instead, ask "what now?" Romans 12:17-19 provides counsel on dealing with difficult situations: "Do not repay anyone evil for evil. Be careful to do what is right in the eyes of everybody. If it is possible, as far as it depends on you, live at peace with everyone. Do not take revenge, my friends, but leave room for God's wrath, for it is written: 'It is mine to avenge; I will repay,' says the Lord."

This humble approach benefited Joshua. Without fail, all his teachers have gone beyond what was expected to help him learn. Our attitude didn't make all the difference. I'm convinced God answered our prayers by placing Joshua with the right teachers. Throughout the years, they made extra efforts like special tutoring, help with notes, and allowing him to take books home.

Teach Personal Accountability

During that time of diagnosis, I had a friend with a son close to Joshua's age. This boy was having trouble of a different kind. He was impulsive and would often get into trouble by defiantly disobeying the teacher. As his mother and I shared stories of our son's challenges, I often heard about how his teacher should just allow these boys to be boys. She talked about how the school should be able to handle her son because that was their job. They needed to figure out how to help him. In the meantime, her son was trying to push mine off the swing set.

Her approach was very defensive and bordered on angry. She was a very devoted mother, but somehow she had passed the responsibility for her son's behavior onto others. I realized that without a change in her attitude, her son would grow up chronically blaming others for his choices.

I committed then and there to teach Joshua personal accountability. While he may have a challenge the other children don't, only he is responsible for how he acts. In reality we all have a challenge called "sin" that draws us away from making loving and respectful choices.

If we aren't careful, our children can use their diagnosis as an excuse for poor behavior. As Christians God calls us to a high level of personal integrity, which means taking responsibility for words and deeds.

Show Unconditional Love

Raising a child with challenging learning needs can be frustrating. At times it pushed us past our tolerance level. We still aren't perfect, but God has given us a greater measure of understanding and patience for Joshua's challenges. While we love our son unconditionally, the truth is we didn't always communicate that. Our frustration sometimes colored the truth within our hearts.

All our children need to know we love them unconditionally, and we should reinforce that with both our actions and words. Yet, a child with a special need—whatever that may be—has an increased need for a parent to affirm that love consistently. Their self-confidence may be shaky when they struggle with what other children call "easy." Having a parent who believes in them, loves them, and is their biggest cheerleader can make the difference between giving up or pressing on.

Memory Verses

*The L*ORD *appeared to us in the past, saying:*
"I have loved you with an everlasting love; I
have drawn you with loving-kindness."

JEREMIAH 31:3

*The L*ORD *gives wisdom, and from his mouth*
come knowledge and understanding.

PROVERBS 2:6

*The L*ORD *will be your confidence and will*
keep your foot from being snared.

PROVERBS 3:26

If it is possible, as far as it depends on
you, live at peace with everyone.

ROMANS 12:18

He guides the humble in what is right
and teaches them his way.

PSALM 25:9

*Show me your ways, O L*ORD, *teach me your paths;*
guide me in your truth and teach me, for you are
God my Savior, and my hope is in you all day long.

PSALM 25:4-5

Encouraging Words

*Some kids feel like they're stupid. I want them to know
that they're not. They just learn differently. Once they
understand that and have the tools to learn in their
individual way, then they can feel good about themselves.*

—CHARLES SCHWAB (DYSLEXIA)

*When I was in my early years (first through fifth grade),
learning disabilities were an unknown entity. Those
of us who had these problems were simply viewed as
unintelligent, and from my perspective the greatest
sadness was that we viewed ourselves the same way.*

—DR. FRED EPSTEIN, NEUROSURGEON (UNDIAGNOSED)

*When you've got something to prove, there's
nothing greater than a challenge.*

—TERRY BRADSHAW (ADHD)

If everyone is thinking alike, then somebody isn't thinking.

—GEORGE PATTON (UNDIAGNOSED)

Discussion or Journal Questions

1. What academic subject does your child enjoy most? Identify
   ways you can encourage this interest outside of your child's
   formal education setting.

2. Identify two or three positive character traits your child dis-
   plays that can benefit his learning. Choose to verbally affirm
   these to your child.

3. What habits would be helpful for your child to develop that would enhance her learning?

4. What personal strengths do you have that can benefit your child's learning? Can you identify ways to help?

5. What are some ways you can make learning fun for your child? Think outside the box or ask others for ideas, and then plan to implement some of these ideas.

6. Identify common mistakes well-meaning parents make when trying to help their children learn.

7. List some of the best ways parents can help their children with learning. These can be practices that have worked for you or practices you've seen others use with success.

8. Have you ever had to be your child's advocate in any situation? Identify what worked and what you would never repeat.

9. It's been said that knowledge is knowing a tomato is a fruit, and wisdom is not putting it in a fruit salad. The Bible tells us both knowledge and wisdom are important. The book of James tells us that God gives wisdom "generously to all without finding fault" (James 1:5). At this point in your child's life, which is more important?

10. Read Psalm 25: 4-5. Spend some time in silent prayer, using these words as a guide. Write down any requests you have of the Lord or anything the Lord reveals to you.

11. What are your greatest needs right now? Write these down. Ask a friend to pray with you and for you regarding these needs.

Chapter Sixteen

Knowing When to Get Professional Help

All the king's horses and all the king's men...

Every parent wonders at times, *Is this behavior normal?* It happens when a normally compliant daughter throws a door-slamming fit. This question pops up when a happy boy sullenly withdraws into his room for hours on end. Toddler tantrums? Prepubescent hormones? Teenage angst? Should a parent ignore the behavior instead of feeding it? Should mom push? Back up? Or give it time and hope the problem works itself out?

Determining what's normal and what's not is every parent's challenge. This is why becoming a student of our children is such an important task. Just as a student attempts to learn everything he can from his teacher or his books, we must become avid learners about our children. Then, when an unusual behavior manifests itself, we are attune to the changes and can respond more appropriately.

This learning pattern begins when our children are babies. We quickly realize that God created each child with a unique temperament. Some children can sleep through anything, while others awaken at the creaking of a door. Some kids can't wait to try something new, while others cling to Mom's leg. These unique characteristics define who we are, and one personality isn't better than another. Although children with certain temperaments are undeniably easier than others for parents to raise, God designed us differently, so that we would complement each other and fulfill His plan here on earth. As parents the more we learn about our child's unique design, the better equipped we are to intervene.

The very fact that you've made it to the end of this book shows you care deeply about the spiritual and emotional needs of your child. It is my prayer that the information found in these chapters, from Scripture, professionals, and other parents, has given you some strategies to help your child with the everyday hurts of life. When we add consistent prayer into our daily lives, I'm convinced there's nothing God can't accomplish and heal.

Even then, occasionally an issue comes along that the most dedicated and caring parents can't solve. When this happens, I believe God might be preparing to answer our prayers through the hands of a professional—especially because we live in a world where the problems are more complicated than when we were children.

Life Is Harder Now

One of my favorite childhood television shows was *The Waltons*. I loved the simplicity of their lives, their kindness to each other, and the commitment to family. Life was much different in rural America in the 1930s. My life growing up in the sixties and seventies was actually simple compared to the life my children face. The problems children faced in earlier decades, while still painful, lacked the violent, stressful edge our kids often face. Because of these dramatic societal changes, our children experience hurts that can go beyond our capacity to help.

Psychiatric nurse practitioner Ann Guthery has daily interaction with children who are impacted by negative changes in today's society. Unfortunately she has also watched it escalate over the past fifteen years. "When I worked in the behavioral health center at a children's hospital in the nineties, we would see teenagers who dealt with suicidal thoughts. Now they're ten- and eleven-year-olds," Guthery said.

"Life is stressful for kids," Guthery continued. "There's an increased emphasis on testing in the school, bullying is worse with more violent threats, and the divorce rate is high. Children thrive on structure and stability when it's in the right place, such as the family." Sadly, however, Guthery notes that many kids lack that healthy structure to withstand the emotional challenges facing them each day.[1]

Even with a healthy structure in place, children are exposed to more violence, crime, sex, and abuse at an earlier age through television and the Internet. I'm sure I'm not the only one to be watching a seemingly harmless program only to be shocked by a commercial for a violent show or an advertisement featuring scantily clad women in undergarments. Just when I think it's safe to go back in the water...

I believe most parents do everything they can to protect their children, but sometimes it just isn't enough. Even with the most loving care and protection, children will deal with something beyond the family's capacity to help. When that happens, consider turning to others for help. Proverbs 15:22 confirms the importance of outside help. "Plans fail for lack of counsel, but with many advisers they succeed."

When a Parent's Help Isn't Enough

Kathy and Brian (names have been changed) are two Christian parents who love their children dearly. As their children grew up, they took care to create a safe and loving home environment where they prioritized their kids' spiritual and emotional health. As professional educators, Kathy and Brian dedicated their professional lives to helping children and were confident in their ability to help their own kids. They enjoyed a picture-perfect family until the day the "wheels fell off" and their son Brandon refused to go to school.

Brandon was a second grader who didn't hate school but didn't love it. Kindergarten and first grade went smoothly enough, but second grade challenged him. Brandon had two teachers who were inflexible, and one was particularly harsh. He told his parents about the teacher but hadn't said much else. As the year progressed, Brandon became more and more afraid of going to school yet wasn't able to communicate why. It had even progressed to the point that Brandon started vomiting before school.

Kathy watched her son resist school and knew something was

wrong, but didn't identify it as a major problem until one morning. "This one day Brandon completely fell apart. He cried and physically resisted going into the school building. I was shocked. Although he hadn't loved school, we hadn't seen anything like that," Kathy said. She talked Brandon into going to school that day by promising to talk with the school counselor, who had earned a reputation as a kind and gentle person.

Brandon grudgingly went to school, and Kathy immediately contacted the counselor. During the course of that day, the counselor brought Brandon into her office. After that meeting Kathy and Brian were called for a meeting. That short one-on-one meeting with the counselor surprised Brandon's parents.

Unbeknownst to them, Brandon's self-esteem had started to suffer because of school. In the course of their meeting, the school counselor asked Brandon about his older brother. Brandon's response revealed volumes about his thoughts. "If you wanted to write my brother's troubles on something, you could use this little chalkboard," he said, pointing to a small blackboard on the table, "but if you wanted to write my troubles, you would have to use this big chalkboard." He finished his statement, as he pointed to the wall.

Brandon had been bottling up his fear of school and his awareness of the differences between his brother and him for months and maybe years. And although Brandon seemed happy-go-lucky for the most part, the truth was he'd been carrying around more burdens than a seven-year-old should.

After learning the depth of Brandon's worries, his parents still tried to handle it on their own, but the fear and physical symptoms, such as throwing up, continued. Kathy and Brian went back to the school counselor, who referred them to a local Christian counselor. It was hard to take that step because, as professional educators, both parents thought they ought to be able to help their son. Thankfully the results were worth reaching out for help.

The professional counselor only met twice with Brandon and then spent the next three months meeting with Kathy and Brian and showing them ways to help their son deal with his anxieties. Instead of pulling Brandon out of school, both the school and private counselor advised keeping him there and dealing head-on with his phobia. They did recommend switching teachers.

In hindsight Kathy realized that as Brandon grew up he had experienced more fears than other children had, but they seemed isolated to her. However, in looking back over Brandon's life, she became aware of the number of ways the family had accommodated the fears instead of dealing with them. "As a mom I just thought he was little, and his fears were no big deal," Kathy said. "Then, when I looked at the whole picture, I realized I had missed something bigger."

Through professional counseling, Kathy and Brian learned how to gradually desensitize Brandon to his fears and teach him coping methods. Today Brandon is a happy and successful fifth grader who only occasionally deals with anxiety.

Although it was an extremely painful time for Brandon and a time of suffering and helplessness for his parents, they are thankful now that it came to such a dramatic head. Kathy summarized, "I became very grateful for the hard time because it revealed a hidden problem. It took it being big for us to wake up to the crisis that could have hindered Brandon from obeying God. Our counselor told me toward the end of our time together, 'What you have done for Brandon is help him so that he can serve God without having to struggle with fear.'"

What Is Normal?

In Brandon's situation, his fear of school manifested itself in physical symptoms until he had a complete breakdown. Up until then his parents thought they were dealing with normal fears connected with this one teacher. Kathy and Brian took immediate action when they realized it was more than a typical childhood reaction to school.

Psychiatric nurse practitioner Ann Guthery counsels that a common red flag for parents is when "loving and soothing your child isn't enough. When a parent can't fill the void, you might need more help."[2] Even then it's hard for parents to identify when a problem has gone beyond their ability to help. This can be due to embarrassment, pride, or disagreement between parents. Not everyone agrees when there is a problem. One parent might think throwing a toy when angry is cause for a psychiatric evaluation, while the other parent might laugh it off as a typical tantrum.

Most counselors who treat adolescents recommend three considerations to determine when a problem needs professional help: the age and gender of the child, the duration of the problem, and the nature of the problem.

Three Considerations

If a child sucks his thumb at age two, it's not a severe problem. But by age ten or twelve, it is a different matter altogether. If your child is still dealing with an issue long after other children his age, it is something to investigate.

Age and Gender of the Child

Sometimes a stressful life change can cause a temporary regression in development. Many children who have passed a developmental milestone, such as potty training, can take a step backward when a younger sibling is born. That's normal and will most often work itself out. However, if the regression is due to witnessing a violent act, your child may need professional intervention. For most life changes, consistent reassurance and love will get your child through a rough spot.

As we consider when a behavior warrants attention, it might be helpful to identify some common behaviors and fears that are normal at different ages.

Infants and Toddlers:

- Fear of loud noises
- Separation anxiety
- Minor defiance (the "mine" syndrome)

Preschoolers:

- Fear of animals, especially dogs
- Fear of the dark
- Fear of make-believe creatures (monsters and ghosts)

School-age:

- Anxiety in a new situation
- Fear of rejection
- Fear of being home alone

Teenagers:

- Desire for independence
- Minor defiance

Just as some behaviors are normal at different ages, some behaviors are normal for different genders. I grew up in a family of four girls, and when God blessed us with three boys, their behavior surprised me—often. My boys did things I never even considered doing as a little girl. I tried asking my mother for advice and just got, "I don't know. You never did that." By then I was convinced of several things. The first was I must have been a perfect child, and the second was God created boys and girls quite differently.

I got to see the comparison between girls and boys firsthand as my friend Becky and I had babies just a few months apart—her first-born was Rachel, and mine was Joshua. Joshua and Rachel grew up as friends. It was great for me to have a friend to talk to about normal baby behavior. Their behavior was very similar in the beginning, except for the fact that Rachel started sleeping through the night much earlier than Josh. However, we soon noticed distinct differences in their God-given design. By age two Joshua was trying to learn to operate the VCR while Rachel could care less about it. Unfortunately Joshua's technological interest involved trying to "play" a sandwich or a Duplo instead of a videotape. They knew me well at the VCR repair shop.

After the third boy was born, my life was a whirlwind of high-energy activity. We didn't do anything at a casual pace. Every walk was a race, and every shopping experience an adventure in mommy-gymnastics. My body contorted beyond normal limits as I corralled a preschooler from running down an aisle, kept a toddler sitting in the cart, and consoled a screaming baby who loudly resented any attempt to confine him for his own safety.

One day I looked at these hopping, bouncing boys and told my husband in complete seriousness, "There is something really wrong with these children!"

My husband didn't skip a beat and answered, "There's nothing wrong with them—they are boys."

So began my journey to discover everyday life with boys. Exploring, daring, and stretching the boundaries of *my* comfort zone became the new "normal." I had to read books about the differences between boys and girls and learn to accept and appreciate how God created men. This might be helpful as you identify behaviors that are outside of your experience. I had to learn that different didn't mean wrong.

I strongly recommend that mothers of boys read *Wild at Heart* by John Eldridge or *Bringing Up Boys* by Dr. James Dobson. Fathers would benefit by reading similar books about girls.

Duration of the Problem

Another reason for concern is the duration of the problem. If you identify something as a problem, such as anger or depression, waiting to deal with it only allows it to grow and ancillary problems to develop. A dripping sink doesn't fix itself—it only wastes water. Some problems won't fix themselves, and our children's hearts are being damaged while we wait.

It is in most of our natures to want to wait and hope that a problem solves itself. The truth is most parents are already running on limited time and energy and can barely manage the day-to-day issues, much less those that are more problematic. Unfortunately children don't always have the coping skills for that to happen. They need intervention, and quickly.

If you identify a new concern that has lasted more than six to eight weeks, it is in your child's best interest to pursue the matter.

That said, some behaviors warrant an immediate response from parents and most likely will require professional help. These include attempts at self-injury, threats of suicide, violent behaviors, or severe withdrawal.

Nature of the Problem

Another reason for increased concern is the nature of the problem. An underlying problem might exist if the child's response to a situation seriously affects his ability to navigate a normal day or there is a noticeable change from normal behavior. The more dramatic, the quicker a parent should respond.

Because every child's "normal" is different, it may be helpful to keep written notes about changes that seem unusual. As Kathy and Brian found out, it's easy to see behaviors as isolated over time, but when viewed from a distance, patterns emerge.

I assembled a list of warning symptoms at different ages. These don't always mean there is a problem requiring professional help, but they are behaviors that should raise our awareness.

Red-Flag Warning Symptoms

Babies and preschool:

- Lack of interest in surroundings
- Lack of appropriate responses
- Severe sleep patterns
- Delays in development

Elementary school age:

- Unable to sit still or read for periods of time

- Sadness that persists over time
- Fear that results in physical symptoms, such as vomiting or shaking
- Constant complaints of physical illness
- Changes in eating or sleeping habits
- Aggressiveness
- Tendency to purposefully annoy and bother others
- Problems that exist in more than one setting
- Decline in grades
- Friends you don't approve of

Teenagers:

- Depression (noted by everyone)
- Excessive sleeping or an inability to sleep for extended periods of time
- Social withdrawal and isolation
- Shift to unusual behavior, basic personality change
- Deterioration of school performance
- Deterioration of social relationships
- Hyperactive or inactive (or alternating between the two)
- Inability to concentrate or cope with minor problems
- Repeated expressions of worthlessness
- Preoccupation with the occult
- Dropping out of activities and out of life in general
- Deterioration and abandonment of personal hygiene
- Attempts to escape through geographic change; frequent moving or hitchhiking trips
- Excessive writing or printing without apparent meaning
- Inappropriate laughter
- Bizarre behavior[3]

Confronting the Brutal Reality of Your Situation

I have an ongoing internal battle with excuses. When I make a mistake, my mind starts frantically searching for an excuse. *Ummm...I forgot because...give me a minute, I'll think of something.* I make excuses for other people too, especially my children. *They didn't mean to do it. It was a one-time thing.* However, excuses are like a bandage on a broken bone—there's no healing of the real problem.

Admitting a problem might exist takes guts. It's much easier to compare our family with another and declare ours to be "pretty good." There might be one issue that's troublesome, but for the most part things are good. Unfortunately, according to management expert Jim Collins, "Good is the enemy of great."[4]

So begins the first chapter of one of the most dynamic business books of the nineties written by Jim Collins. In *Good to Great*, Collins and a team of researchers set out to discover what turns a good company into a great company. It took five years of research and processing to uncover the universal distinguishing characteristics of companies that became great performers over time. Turns out it isn't companies on the cutting edge of technology or those with charismatic leaders. Rather great companies exhibit long-term, consistently good leadership and smart practices.

My husband and I both read the book, thinking it would be helpful for us as we run our two home-based companies. About halfway through the book, my husband had a brilliant thought: *What if we applied these good-to-great principles to our family? Could we take our good family and make it great? If so, what would it take from us?*

While reading the book, we discovered that the steps to a great company started with having a determined yet humble leader and the right people "on the bus." God had already picked the leader and decided who would be on our family bus. So the next most important step in launching to greatness is confronting the brutal facts about the reality of the situation. This involves an honest and diligent effort to uncover the truth plus creating an environment where people are comfortable speaking and hearing the truth.

Most of us resist admitting there is a problem—especially if it involves us. If we do admit there's a problem, accepting the depth of the problem is hard. However, according to Collins, "When you start with an honest and diligent effort to determine the truth of your situation, the right decisions often become self-evident. It is impossible to make good decisions without infusing the entire process with an honest confrontation of the brutal facts."[5]

Helping our children most effectively takes the same brutal confrontation of the truth. I'll never forget the resistance I heard from other parents as my husband and I were trying to figure out why our eldest son couldn't sit still in class when every other child sat attentively or why he was off task in math 85 percent of the time.

The suggestions ran from it was the teacher's fault to boys will be boys. And yet the nagging in my heart that something was different about this boy wouldn't stop. When a school psychologist's evaluation revealed Josh's atypicality was off the charts, I knew we were dealing with something besides just a normal active boy.

Everything within me wanted to agree that the teacher should just figure out how to work with Josh as he was. Realistically Josh needed special help, and accepting that fact propelled us into action.

Confirm This Reality with Other Adults in Your Child's Life

If you suspect there might be a problem, talk with the other adults in your child's life. This could include his or her school teachers, teachers and leaders at church, physicians, coaches, relatives, scout leaders, and so on. This will give you an idea if the problem is widespread or isolated. If a child exhibits normal behavior at school but changes drastically at home, perhaps it's best to make changes in the home environment before professionally addressing the issue.

Steps to Take

Praying, I believe, is the first step we should take when there is an inkling of a problem. Pray for your child and with your child. Ask members of your church and small group to pray. Consider taking your child to others and having them lay hands and pray over your child. We have direct access to the throne of God, the Creator of the universe, and the Master Designer of us, and we should boldly ask God for help. After all, no one loves or wants to help your child more than God.

A second step would be to visit your pediatrician or family physician. This way you can identify if you are actually dealing with a physical problem that could manifest itself in a behavioral issue. If you eliminate a physical issue, then your physician should be a good resource for other community help. The school therapist or counselor should be able to offer referrals as well. Specifically request a Christian counselor so you can deal with the spiritual issues as well as the emotional ones.

There Is Hope

Satan's most effective tool to minimize a parent's effectiveness and zeal is to plant seeds of despair. I know because I have fought these thoughts in difficult times. Fear left me shaking, worry stole the joy from my day, and helplessness overwhelmed me. Yet in the midst of the darkness, God's unchanging promises helped me through. When doubt threatens, I stand not on my own strength but on the truth of God's Word. God tells me this about my children:

- He loves them (John 3:16).
- He has a plan that cannot be thwarted (Psalm 57:2-3, Job 42:2).
- He is working for their good (Romans 8:28).
- He will answer their call for help (Psalm 91).
- He won't abandon them in times of trouble (Deuteronomy 31:8).

Satan would like to turn our problems into reasons to doubt God. God, on the other hand, already has a plan for how to use our problems and those our children are facing to bring good into our lives and advance His kingdom. If we could discipline ourselves to look beyond this current bump in the road with anticipation, if we could believe that God is going to do something great, we would give Satan no entry point to work in our lives.

Getting professional help for a challenge your child faces is the beginning of something amazing God already has planned. Rest in peace, my sweet sister or brother. Although we will face trouble in this life, Jesus has already won!

Memory Verses

*I have told you these things, so that in me you may
have peace. In this world you will have trouble.
But take heart! I have overcome the world.*

JOHN 16:33

*I know that you can do all things; no
plan of yours can be thwarted.*

JOB 42:2

*The LORD himself goes before you and will be
with you; he will never leave you nor forsake you.
Do not be afraid; do not be discouraged.*

DEUTERONOMY 31:8

*And we know that in all things God works
for the good of those who love him, who have
been called according to his purpose.*

ROMANS 8:28

*When Jesus woke up, he rebuked the wind and said
to the water, "Silence! Be still!" Suddenly the wind
stopped, and there was a great calm. Then he asked
them, "Why are you afraid? Do you still have no faith?"*

MARK 4:39-40 NLT

Encouraging Words

Adversity reveals genius, prosperity conceals it.

—Horace

A smooth sea never made a skilled mariner.

—English Proverb

You gain strength, experience and confidence by every experience where you really stop to look fear in the face. You must do the thing you cannot do.

—Eleanor Roosevelt

Discussion or Journal Questions

1. It seems to be human nature to either exaggerate or minimize a problem. Do you find yourself leaning in one of these directions?

2. How would you define a great family?

3. What are some of the challenges your family faces as you consider moving from a good family to a great family? How can you overcome them?

4. What are some ways you can identify "normal" for your child?

5. What are some reasons you might resist taking your child to counseling or to receive other professional help?

6. Do you think most children are prepared to handle the problems this world presents to them at an early age? Is there

anything you can do as a parent to help prepare your child now so they aren't overwhelmed later?

7. Is there any nagging concern you have regarding your child's behavior or response to a situation? If so, share that with someone and commit to seeking wise counsel.

8. Sometimes a child's actions cause us to despair. If your child has acted inappropriately, remind yourself of the good you have seen in your child. Make a list of all the good qualities you know your child possesses.

9. When you feel despair over your child's situation, what brings you peace and reassurance?

10. Read Deuteronomy 31:8. What comfort does this truth bring?

Chapter One: The Difference a Parent Makes

1. Dr. James Dobson, *The New Hide or Seek* (Grand Rapids, MI: Fleming H. Revell, 1999), p. 105.

Chapter Two: Dealing with Disappointment

1. Liberty Savard, *Shattering Your Strongholds* (Gainesville, FL: Bridge-Logos Publishers, 1992), p. 27.

Chapter Three: When Words Hurt

1. Sharon Jaynes, *The Power of a Woman's Words* (Eugene, OR: Harvest House Publishers, 2007), p. 24.
2. Rabbi Joseph Telushkin, *Words That Hurt, Words That Heal* (New York, NY: William Morrow and Company, 1996) p. 101.
3. Rabbi Joseph Telushkin, *Words That Hurt, Words That Heal*, p. 104.
4. Gary Smalley and John Trent, Ph.D., *The Blessing* (New York, NY: Simon & Schuster Inc., 1986), p. 27.
5. Les Parrott III, Ph.D., *High Maintenance Relationships* (Carol Stream, IL: Tyndale House Publishers, 1997), p. 236.

Chapter Four: Overcoming Fear

1. Williams Sears, M.D., "7 Ways to Help Your Child Handle Fear," *A to Z Index,* http://www.askdrsears.com/html/10/t110248.asp.
2. John S. Dacey and Lisa B. Fiore, *Your Anxious Child* (San Francisco, CA: Jossey-Bass, Inc., 2000), p. 142.
3. John Ortberg, *If You Want to Walk on Water, You've Got to Get Out of the Boat* (Grand Rapids, MI: Zondervan, 2001), p. 118.
4. John Ortberg, *If You Want to Walk on Water, You've Got to Get Out of the Boat*, p. 121.

Chapter Five: Managing Stress

1. "Top Triggers For Stress in Children," *Clinical Psychiatry News*, January 2006, p. 40.
2. Georgia Witkin, Ph.D., *KidStress* (New York, NY: Viking Penguin, 1999), p. 63.
3. Georgia Witkin, Ph.D., *KidStress*, pp. 61-63.
4. Mary Southerland, *Escaping the Stress Trap* (Eugene, OR: Harvest House Publishers, 2006), p. 13.
5. Rick Warren, *The Purpose-Driven Life* (Grand Rapids, MI: Zondervan, 2002), p. 31.

6. David Allen, *Getting Things Done* (New York, NY: Penguin Group, 2001), pp. 4-5.
7. David Allen, *Getting Things Done*, p. 23.

Chapter Six: The Pain of Loneliness

1. Faculty of Harvard Medical School, "Making Connections Good for the Heart and Soul," *Harvard Heart Letter* (January 2007), p. 5.
2. Hara Estroff Marano, *Why Doesn't Anybody Like Me?* (New York, NY: William Morrow and Company, 1998), p. 5.
3. Hara Estroff Marano, *Why Doesn't Anybody Like Me?*, p. 238.
4. Dr. James Dobson, *The New Hide or Seek* (Grand Rapids, MI: Fleming H. Revell, 1999), p. 27.
5. Tim Hansel, *Through the Wilderness of Loneliness* (Elgin, IL: David C. Cook Publishing Co., 1991), p. 29.

Chapter Seven: Turning Failure into Victory

1. Verla Gillmor, "Facing Failure," *Today's Christian Woman*, May/June 2001, Vol. 23, No. 3, p. 66.

Chapter Eight: Body Awarenss

1. Edward J. Cumella, Ph.D., "Eating Disorders: An Introduction," *Eating Disorder Articles,* www.remudaranch.com/articles/eating_disorders_an_introduction/index.php.
2. Remuda Ranch, "Eating Disorder Myths," www.remudaranch.com.
3. William J. Richardson, Ph.D., *Loving Obedience* (Chicago, IL: Northfield Publishing, 2000), p. 19.
4. NIV Study Bible, 10th Anniversary Edition (Grand Rapids, MI: Zondervan Publishing House, 1984), p. 1001-1002.
5. Ginger Plowman, *Don't Make Me Count to Three* (Wapwallopen, PA: Shepherd Press, 2003), p. 36.
6. Carol Brazo, *No Ordinary Home* (Sisters, OR: Multnomah Books 1995), pp. 24-25.

Chapter Nine: Hope After Loss: Dealing with Grief

1. Marlo Francis, interviewed by author, May 2007.
2. Joyce Meyers, "Overcoming Grief and Loneliness," *Everyday Answers*, http://www.joycemeyer.org/OurMinistries/EverydayAnswers/Articles/art15.htm.

Chapter Ten: Anger: When Is It Wrong?

1. Tim LaHaye, *Spirit-Controlled Temperament* (Wheaton, IL: Tyndale House, 1992), p. 130.
2. Search for "orge" in the Lexicons in Bible Study Tools at crosswalk.com, http://biblestudy.crosswalk.com/search/default.aspx?keyword=orge&type=library&category-Lexicons.
3. Dan Russ, *Flesh-and-Blood Jesus* (Grand Rapids, MI: Baker Books 2008), p. 118.
4. Les Carter, *Getting the Best of Your Anger* (Grand Rapids, MI: Fleming H. Revell, 2006), p. 35.
5. Tim LaHaye, *Spirit-Controlled Temperament*, p. 140.

6. Karen L. Maudlin, Psy.D., "The Angry Child," *Christian Parenting Today*, March/April 2001, Vol. 13, No. 4, p. 38.

7. Michael R. Emlet, M.Div., M.D., *Angry Children* (Greensboro, NC: New Growth Press, 2008), p. 5.

8. Ginger Plowman, *Don't Make Me Count to Three* (Wapwallopen, PA: Shepherd Press, 2003), p. 40.

9. William J. Richardson, Ph.D., *Loving Obedience* (Chicago, IL: Northfield Publishing, 2000), p. 146.

10. William J. Richardson, Ph.D., *Loving Obedience*, p. 147.

Chapter Eleven: Investing in Your Child's Strengths

1. Rick Warren, *The Purpose-Driven Life* (Grand Rapids, MI: Zondervan, 2002), p. 235.

Chapter Twelve: Overcoming Insecurity

1. Dr. James Dobson, *The New Hide or Seek* (Grand Rapids, MI: Fleming H. Revell, 1999), p. 27.

2. Dr. Kevin Leman, *Bringing Up Kids Without Tearing Them Down* (New York, NY: Delacorte Press, 1993), p. 6.

3. Timothy R. Jennings, M.D., *Could It Be This Simple?* (Hagerstown, MD: Autumn House Publishing, 2007), p 39-40.

Chapter Thirteen: Dealing with a Bully

1. Paul Coughlin, *No More Jellyfish, Chickens, or Wimps* (Bloomington, MN: Bethany House Publishers, 2007), p. 147.

2. Elin McCoy, *What to Do When Kids Are Mean to Your Child* (Pleasantville, NY/Montreal: Pen and Pencil Books, LLC, 1997), p. 29.

3. Paul Coughlin, *No More Jellyfish, Chickens, or Wimps*, p. 137.

Chapter Fifteen: When Your Child Learns Differently

1. B. Bloom and R.A. Cohen, "Summary Health Statistics for U.S. Children: National Health Interview Survey, 2006." National Center for Health Statistics. Vital Health Stat 10(234). 2007.

Chapter Sixteen: Knowing When to Get Professional Help

1. Ann Guthery, interview by author, March 7. 2008.

2. Ann Guthery, interview by author, March 7. 2008.

3. Parents Involved Network, "Teenagers," *Does Your Child Need Help?*, www.pinofpa.org/resources/child_help_b.html.

4. Jim Collins, *Good to Great* (New York, NY: HarperCollins Publishers, Inc., 2001), p. 1.

5. Jim Collins, *Good to Great*, p. 88.

To learn more about books by Harvest House Publishers
or to read sample chapters, log on to our website:

www.harvesthousepublishers.com

HARVEST HOUSE PUBLISHERS

EUGENE, OREGON